# Pride of the Morning
## An Oxford Childhood

# Pride of the Morning
## An Oxford Childhood

Phyl Surman

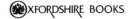
OXFORDSHIRE BOOKS

ALAN SUTTON

First published in the United Kingdom in 1992 by
Alan Sutton Publishing Ltd • Phoenix Mill • Far Thrupp
Stroud • Gloucestershire
in association with
Oxfordshire Books • Oxfordshire County Council • Leisure and Arts

First Published in the United States of America in 1992 by
Alan Sutton Publishing Inc • Wolfeboro Falls • NH 03896-0848

British Library Cataloguing in Publication Data

Surman, Phyl
Pride of the Morning
I. Title
942. 574082092

ISBN 0-7509-0146-2


Library of Congress Cataloging in Publication Data applied for

*Cover photograph:* Children playing 'ducks and drakes' in the sheep-washing
place, Barracks Lane, Cowley, July 1914.

Typeset in 11/12 Bembo.
Typesetting and origination by
Alan Sutton Publishing Limited.
Printed in Great Britain by
The Bath Press, Bath, Avon.

*Youth is the morning
of life, let it be
remembered with pride*

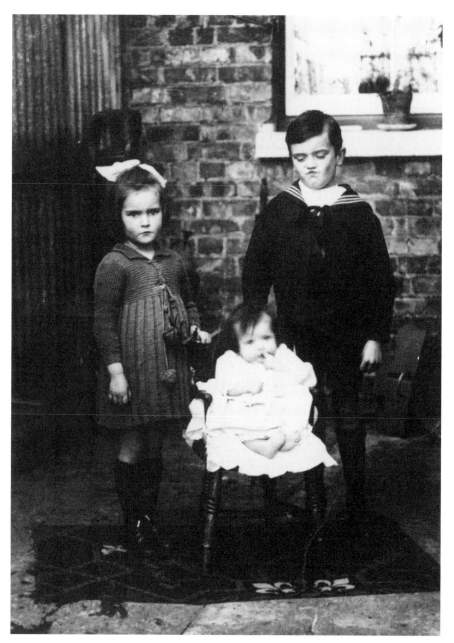

'We three children'

# CONTENTS

# FOREWORD

Historians are drawn to Oxford like moths to a flame but their work rarely does much to record the daily lives of ordinary folk. In *Pride of the Morning,* Phyl Surman does something to redress the balance, bringing us vivid memories of her east Oxford childhood in the 1920s. She broadcast regularly on BBC Radio Oxford in the 1970s and the infectious enthusiasm which she displayed 'on air' is also present in her writing, catapulting us straight back into a very different world.

Phyllis (or Phyl), the elder daughter of Harry and Alma Beck, was born in 1917. Her father was a plumber who had married Alma Haynes in 1913 and, at a time when most people still rented property, they were struggling to buy the family home, no. 74 Howard Street, on a mortgage. Phyl had an older brother, Norman, who was born in 1914 and a younger sister, Joyce, born in 1921.

*Pride of the Morning* recalls a happy and secure childhood centred around a home which served as 'my refuge, to which, at the losing end of a battle with other children, I could return to continue a shouted argument through the keyhole of its strong front door'. Like many east Oxford families, the Becks were far from prosperous and Phyl was ten years old before her parents could afford to take her on a seaside holiday. Nevertheless, Harry was in regular employment and, if plumbing work was in short supply, he was also a trained metal-worker. He was therefore in a position to subscribe to the Cutler Boulter Provident Dispensary in Marston Street which offered medical treatment to the family in the event of illness; he also contributed to the Independent Order of Oddfellows which would provide financial help if the breadwinner became ill or incapacitated.

The family enjoyed day excursions by river steamer or charabanc and went for long walks in the fields beyond Iffley. In most years, they were able to take cheap summer holidays in leafy Warwickshire where Aunt Eva's husband was chauffeur to a wealthy lady. All the year round, the children used the traffic-free east Oxford streets as a joyful playground, although they exasperated a near-neighbour on the corner of Catherine Street by their noisy games.

They had a recreation ground nearby in Cowley Road and further afield they could explore Shotover and the rural fringes of Cowley.

At the age of four, Phyl went to SS Mary and John Infants' School in Hertford Street and then, three years later, to the big school next door. This two-storey building was ingeniously designed with the girls entering from Essex Street to the first floor and the boys from Hertford Street to the ground floor. Segregation of the sexes was also practised at the Becks' local church, St Alban's, although 'this did not prevent the exchange of grimaces, some smirking, some threatening, across the central aisle'. St Alban's was High Church and the children were impressed for a while by the pageantry of the service before settling down to swap 'treasured pieces of silver paper with our neighbour'.

Gradually, Phyl's local perspectives widened and, in 1927, she gained a scholarship which enabled her to go to the Central Girls' School in New Inn Hall Street. The avid observer of local shops in and around the Cowley Road could now gaze in wonder at the delights of the Penny Bazaar in St Ebbe's or perhaps have tea with her parents in the Cadena Café.

Phyl Surman completed *Pride of the Morning* in 1978 and a few of her contemporary remarks have inevitably been overtaken by subsequent events. Parsons' Pleasure, the well-known bathing place for men on the river Cherwell has now been closed; so too has the Long Bridges bathing place where she spent so many happy hours. On the corner of Catherine Street and Howard Street the 'Slipper Baths' closed in 1978 after bathrooms had been installed in most local houses. Change goes on, but the east Oxford of Phyl's childhood will always be found in these memories. Phyl Surman died in 1985 and *Pride of the Morning* is published by kind permission of her son, David.

Malcolm Graham

# ACKNOWLEDGEMENTS

With grateful thanks to all who have assisted in the production of this book, especially:

Mr F. Ackerman; Mr R. Angus; Mr W.E. Arthy; Mr N.G. Beck; Mrs J. Blakeman; Mr R.D. Burnell; Mr C. Clarke; Mr T. Colverson; Mr V. Couling; Revd E.H.W. Crusha; Dr M. Graham; Mr J.R. Hunt; Mr L. Lardner; Revd Arnold Mallinson; Mr W.J. Rose; Mr A.R. Sargent; Society of St John the Evangelist; Mr T.J. Surman; Mr J.M. Surman; Thames Water Authority; Mr M.A. Tredwell; Revd Canon A.G. Whye; Mrs W. Crook; Mrs U. Scrivyer; Mrs M. Knight.

Photographs are reproduced courtesy of David Surman, Jeremy Daniels and Oxfordshire Photographic Archives. The drawings are by Max Surman.

CHAPTER ONE

# OUR HOUSE

In 1920, development along the eastern side of Iffley Road in east Oxford ceased with three long, straight streets: Percy Street, Charles Street and Howard Street. From Howard Street, halfway along its western side, Catherine Street branched out extending to Magdalen Road, cutting through Percy and Charles Streets on its way, so that they were each divided into two unequal lengths, the shorter of which were known as 'Little Percy Street' and 'Little Charles Street'.

Several theories have been put forward as to why these three streets were so named, the most likely of which appears to be that, in the 1860s to 1870s, a William Howard was living with his family on the Iffley Road and, being an estate agent, it is conceivable that he may have been involved in the development of this area. The census of 1871 shows that he had six children, the youngest of whom, then aged five years, was named Percy; none of the other five was called Charles, but there may have been another son of that name who died in infancy. Alternatively, there may have been some other reason why the name Charles should have been chosen. By 1871, Percy, Charles and Howard streets were all laid out and building was in progress. Percy Street had six houses, two of them uninhabited; Charles Street had twenty-six houses, one unoccupied; and Howard Street, nine houses, of which five were empty. At the time of which I write the three streets were completely built up and, beyond, allotments and fields stretched away to Iffley Turn. To locals this area was known as 'Robin Hood', and was zealously guarded by the younger element of the community who met any threat of invasion of their territory by rival gangs with cries of 'Up Robin Hood!' As to why our neighbourhood was so called, correspondence in the *Oxford Mail* dated 9 September 1976 suggests that the name resulted from the existence in Magdalen Road of a public house of that title, but earlier correspondence in the newspaper quotes from the parish magazine of July 1915:

At that time [the early fifties] and for years before an encampment of gipsies had settled on the site of what was later 'Robin Hood Terrace' and, as is usual, they had great difficulty in removing them. It was from this that the district derived the name of 'Robin Hood'.

I was also intrigued by the following statement in the Cowley St John parish magazine dated January 1920: 'Father Jacob has taken charge of "London over the Border", i.e., the part of the parish the other side of Iffley Road.' This was the first and only reference I came across to what was presumably a local name for the area lying to the west of the main road to Iffley.

Our house was situated about halfway down Howard Street, which, though straight, displayed no monotony in the buildings lining its footpaths. Some were terraced, a few three storeys high, others, like ours, semi-detached with a side entrance, but all boasted a small front garden about ten feet deep enclosed in most cases by railings and a privet hedge. Entrance to our house was by means of a side door; glass panelled, stained and grained to a high polish it surmounted two steps, one of stone, scrubbed daily, and another of brass, polished daily. This door opened into a small hall, the consequent rush of air causing small rectangles of coloured glass suspended from the ceiling to tinkle a musical welcome. Directly opposite the main entrance lay the door to the front room, to the left, the door to the living room and, far left, the staircase leading to the three bedrooms.

The front room enlarged by a bay window was used only for parties, visitors, or sometimes on Sundays. The windows were hung with white lace

Howard Street in 1906 - home of the author

2

curtains and two heavy green curtains suspended from wooden rings on a pole and looped back to either side of the bay in which stood, the pride of most households, a bamboo stand holding a monster aspidistra plant. The furniture in this room consisted of a horsehair sofa, one end of which curled up high, as a pillow, while along its back ran a small wooden balustrade; there were four matching chairs and the wallpaper was deep red. In this room stood an upright mahogany piano with two brass candlesticks hinged to its satin-backed fretwork facing; this instrument, much used and loved by my brother Norman, held little interest for me; the truth was that I found the practice sessions boring and consequently made laborious progress.

The fireplace was of black marble with red tiles, and the hearth was surrounded by a brass fender on which reposed brass fire-irons. The doors, skirting and other woodwork were painted dark brown, it being then considered that dark colours were more practical.

Most of the woodwork in the living room was painted dark green, the doors panelled and low-handled in brass. The mantelshelf was draped with green material edged with bobbles, and on the shelf stood a large mirror flanked by two tall, narrow mirrors reflecting a framework of small shelves holding ornaments. A plain deal table stood in the centre of the room covered with a bobble-edged cloth to match the mantelshelf, and on the floor lay a rag rug made by my mother from strips of thick material threaded into hessian with a wooden peg. For some weeks before attempting such a task she would ask around our friends and relations for cast-off coats or thick curtains which might be cut up for this purpose, so that when the completed rug finally lay before the hearth, we children would sit on it and, selecting a strip, amuse ourselves by recounting the history of its source:

'That's Uncle Ern's post office coat.'

'That was mum's old dressing gown, and look, that piece of red was your old gaiters!'

In the centre of the ceiling was suspended a gas jet with a voracious appetite for mantles; I was constantly being sent round to a nearby shop for replacements for they were easily shattered. The fireplace was an 'oven and sham', black-leaded and surrounded by a steel fender and fire-irons which were covered with newspaper on bath nights so that as we dried off before the fire there was no fear of splashing and staining these objects.

Hardly a house in this area had the luxury of a bathroom, but my father, who was a very practical man, had fitted a bath into the kitchen with a wooden cover which served as a table. Water for baths was heated in a corner copper under which a fire was lit, and when the water was hot it was bucketed across the kitchen and poured into the bath. Sheets and linens were all home laundered and boiled in the copper for there were then few organised laundries, though some women had wash-houses built in their gardens and took in washing, either from neighbours or from the Oxford colleges, to augment their income. Later, these brick coppers which took up so much space in the kitchen were removed and replaced by gas or electric boilers, but there were no airing facilities in winter, so that it was common in many homes to find the living-room criss-crossed with string on which washing or airing seemed almost permanently hung, for the weekly wash was a mammoth task. My mother was very much against this practice and our things were aired on a large wooden clothes-horse which she placed in the warm living-room last thing at night.

The oven and sham ranges in the living-room also began to lose favour about this time, being replaced by open coal grates with tiled surrounds and wooden mantelpieces, and cooking was then performed on kitchen ranges, though these too were soon replaced by gas stoves and later still, electric ovens. Despite the obvious advantages of these ovens, being easier to clean and control, my mother still favoured the coal range. Opening its oven door, she would hold her hand inside to test the heat and somehow she knew just when to put in her sandwiches and pies, and baking-day in our house was always warm and golden. On the front of most ranges was a grid iron on which flat irons were heated, usually two; one was heated while the other was in use, so that no time was lost. The iron handles were, of course, hot, and for this purpose, by the side of the range hung a padded iron or kettle-holder. These holders were the first things that we were taught to make in the sewing class at school.

Utensils were made of tinned metal or enamel and kitchen buckets, baths etc. usually of galvanised metal, though enamelled hip-baths were still in use. Saucepans were of iron and very heavy, but when the new stoves came into being, lighter models of enamel or aluminium pans were used. Behind the kitchen door stood a large wooden mangle with cupboards beneath and further cupboard space was provided under the stairs.

The upstairs rooms were lit by gas, but here, no mantle, just a hinged bracket ending with a bare half circle of flame which could be turned down to a small blue glimmer once we were in bed. My bedroom had a brass bedstead with mattress of flock filling, hard and lumpy, but with experience I learned to fit my body quite comfortably into its undulations. There was a dressing-table covered with a lace duchesse set, a wardrobe and a marble-topped wash-hand stand, complete with jug, basin and soap-dish, and on the wall over the fireplace hung a large coloured picture of *The Light of the World*, by William Holman Hunt. My father, who usually rose first in the morning, would bring warm water upstairs for us but he would get washed and shaved in the kitchen.

This, then, was my home around 1920, kept clean and in good repair by

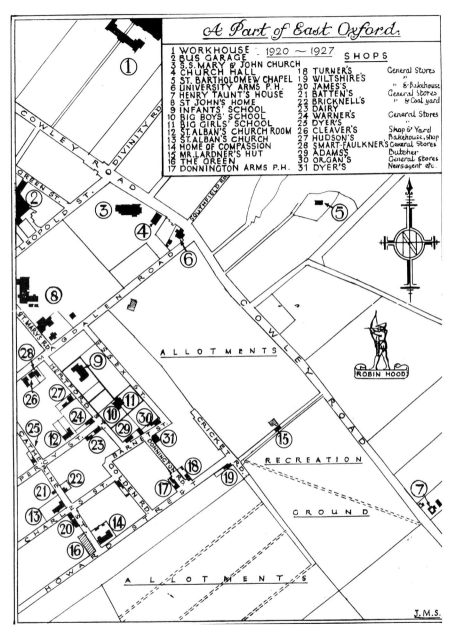

**A Part of East Oxford.**

1920 ~ 1927

1 WORKHOUSE
2 BUS GARAGE
3 S.S. MARY & JOHN CHURCH
4 CHURCH HALL
5 ST. BARTHOLOMEW CHAPEL
6 UNIVERSITY ARMS P.H.
7 HENRY TAUNT'S HOUSE
8 ST JOHN'S HOME
9 INFANTS' SCHOOL
10 BIG BOYS' SCHOOL
11 BIG GIRLS' SCHOOL
12 ST. ALBAN'S CHURCH ROOM
13 ST. ALBAN'S CHURCH
14 HOME OF COMPASSION
15 MR. LARDNER'S HUT
16 THE GREEN
17 DONNINGTON ARMS P.H.

SHOPS

| | |
|---|---|
| 18 TURNER'S | General Stores |
| 19 WILTSHIRE'S | " |
| 20 JAMES'S | " & Bakehouse |
| 21 BATTEN'S | General Stores |
| 22 BRICKNELL'S | " & Coal yard |
| 23 DAIRY | |
| 24 WARNER'S | General Stores |
| 25 DYER'S | " |
| 26 CLEAVER'S | Shop & Yard |
| 27 HUDSON'S | Bakehouse, shop |
| 28 SMART-FAULKNER'S | General Stores |
| 29 ADAMS'S | Butcher |
| 30 ORGAN'S | General Stores |
| 31 DYER'S | Newsagent etc. |

ROBIN HOOD

J.M.S.

A part of east Oxford

5

my hardworking parents. They had little money when they married in 1913, but had managed to buy this house for £250, most of which they borrowed and were still repaying. Sublimely unaware of financial problems, I regarded this house as security, my refuge, to which, at the losing end of a battle with other children, I could retire to continue a shouted argument through the keyhole of its strong front door. I also had complete faith in my parents. In my childish estimation there was nothing they could not do or provide and this feeling was obviously shared by my brother, for he recalls taking home six of his school friends one day calmly announcing to my surprised mother that they had 'come to tea'. Father could be relied upon to repair bicycle punctures and mend broken toys and he knew the best places to fish for minnows or to seek out the yellow king-cup; and oh, the comfort of my mother who was always there and understood how to deal with cut knees and sums which would not add up! To my parents I turned for reassurance when angry or upset, or for practical advice; I accepted their caring presence as a normal part of my existence, never thinking there could come a time when I might be deprived of their support, so that when, in later years, they inevitably became old, ill and uncertain, it was with a feeling of shock that I realized that they too were mortal.

The front gate step of this house was my favourite resting-place where I might sit (despite its coldness to my bottom and the sinister warning from Norman that I should 'catch the quack') happily meditating and watching the world go by. It was while so engaged one autumn morning, pensively munching an apple, that I remembered uneasily the unpleasant task I had allocated for that day. In the evening there was to be a 'pig-killing', so this morning I must say 'Good-bye' to Blackie and Whitey.

In common with many householders my father kept chickens in a wire-netted run and two pigs in a sty at the bottom of our garden. Pig-sties were allowed only in gardens on the eastern side of Howard Street because they were backed by allotments and this meant that the sty was sufficiently far away from human habitation to comply with the law. The pigs were, in fact, the joint property of several neighbours who contributed to their feeding. Acorns, household scraps, small rejected 'tatties' were all boiled together in a big, black iron saucepan and greedily enjoyed by the animals, blissfully unaware that, at the end of the year, the donors of this gastronomic mess would come to assist at the killing and apportionment of the carcasses. Nothing was wasted. The pig skin or flare was melted down for lard; the blood drained from the carcass used to make black puddings; the innards boiled down for faggots, and chitterlings and trotters were dishes in their own right. The pig's head was often made into brawn and the hams and choice portions treated with saltpetre and stored away for winter eating.

The necessity for this butchery had been gently explained to me by father: 'It's the way of the world I'm afraid, dear. We must kill animals to live.'

But I always hated the killings and so it was with heavy heart that I walked round to the back garden, hoping, perhaps, that a little explanatory chat might be of some consolation to the pigs. Our garden was of useful size and accommodated a pear tree, four apple trees, a damson tree and currant and gooseberry bushes, with a small lawn and flower garden near the house. Honeysuckle threaded itself on a trellis near the back door and the perfume from this on a still summer evening was exquisite. But the glories of the garden were lost upon me as, in this moment of sadness, I walked slowly past the chicken run; even they, I thought dismally, will meet a similar fate, yet they served us well and in addition to our own needs we often sold eggs to neighbours, preserving the surplus in a big crock of water-glass for winter use. These same chickens had been reared from the shell in a large flannel-lined box which was placed in a warm spot in the hearth; a yellow fluff-ruffled, cheeping mass among which one occasionally saw a small amber claw or bright beady eye and there they stayed until strong enough to face the world outside. I decided it would be kinder not to enlighten them and left them clucking and pecking to their hearts' content.

At the bottom of the garden leaned 'Dad's shed'; a construction of planks and corrugated iron held together by long nails which, when hammered home, went right through the planks, so forming a useful hook on the inside of the shed for coils of wire or bunches of keys. My mother always vowed that had it not been for the contents this structure would have collapsed and, indeed, it did appear that walls and roof were kept in place by the many biscuit tins and rows of shelving stacked internally. Tins full of rusty nuts and bolts, nails, odd door furniture, washers, screws, and on the shelves, tools, pieces of piping, tins of putty, bottles of methylated spirits and cans of paraffin were to be seen in glorious disarray. On the bench below the only window, a vice, soldering-irons, flux and miscellaneous tools were always in evidence, and beneath the bench, odd sheets of glass, tin, copper and pieces of lead. Yet this cluttered, crazy workshop housed the remedy for many a crisis of maintenance; whatever was needed was to be found in 'Dad's shed'. That is until, in later years, my tidy-minded brother took a hand and put the place in order. Tools were put into racks, tins and boxes neatly labelled, the bench cleared and rubbish thrown away, after which my father complained he could not find a thing!

To the right of the shed was a cycle shed and to the left, the object of my thoughts, the pig-sty. Perched up on the wooden fence around the sty and adopting what I considered to be a soothing tone, I attempted to explain to Blackie and Whitey that their sacrifice was all very necessary because Dad had said so. In my anxiety to get this message across I leaned too far over, lost my footing, and found myself hanging upside down, my face inches away from the bewhiskered, pink, snuffling nostrils of Whitey. The indignity of my position was quite outweighed by the alarming proximity of the pig and I was convinced that far from grieving over the threat of his own demise, Whitey was about to relish the last meal of the condemned! My piercing shrieks brought mother running from the kitchen and she, locating the sound, perceived two short fat legs protruding from navy-blue fleecy-lined boots above the sty door. Laughing, she uprighted me and together we left the pig to ruminate on the peculiarities of humans.

Later that night, when the darkness was pierced by the light of many lanterns and the quietness shattered by men's voices and the shrill screams of the pigs, I lay with my head under the bedclothes, fingers in ears, and wept for Blackie and Whitey.

# CHAPTER TWO

# THE NEIGHBOURHOOD

Soon after this sad incident, I was cheered by the news that there was to be a wedding in the family. My mother's sister May was to be married to Pat and the whole family was invited to the ceremony at SS Mary and John church on 19 September 1920.

This was to be a great event. I was to have a new fawn coat and brown velvet hat decorated with buttercups made by my mother, as were all my clothes, and Norman was to be resplendent in a new sailor suit. On the appointed day, we assembled with other relatives in the big church and I was allowed to sit at the end of the pew so that I might more easily watch the proceedings, but this did not satisfy my curiosity. I could see my aunt May and my prospective uncle Pat standing before the vicar, but, being unable to hear what was said or see what was happening, I left my seat, avoiding father's outstretched hand, walked down the aisle and pushing between bride and groom came face to face with the reverend gentleman. Startled though he must have been, he did not falter and the ceremony proceeded with the interloper maintaining her position throughout.

Afterwards there was a wedding breakfast at Granny's house in Temple Street, to which Norman and I did full justice, and then the newlyweds left to spend their honeymoon with aunt Eva, another of mother's sisters, at Ashorne in Warwickshire. How I wished there could be weddings every day: I enjoyed the happiness, the flowers, the food and above all, the family atmosphere. This sense of belonging, that my brother and I were the pivot of my parents' world, must have been instilled since my earliest days and it was, therefore, probably a good thing that in 1921, a new member of the family arrived, Joyce, born during the hot month of August. She, being rather a delicate infant, needed a great deal of attention, particularly when, at the age of a few months, she developed pneumonia and almost died. Her cot was brought downstairs so that mother could watch her constantly, snatching fitful sleep in a chair by the cot side during the long hours of night. Though only four years old, I was conscious of the anxiety and fetched and carried for my mother, who hardly left the baby. Fortunately, this care and devotion was eventually rewarded and Joyce slowly recovered. Infant mortality at this time was very high and month by month church records of burials show the sad entries: aged one hour; aged ten hours; aged five weeks; and register the deaths of many young people.

Neighbours were very kind to us during this crisis, and would undertake shopping or have me to play with their children to relieve my mother. On one such occasion, playing with a neighbour's child, I followed her indoors and found myself in a dimly lit room wherein several children played and in one corner of which, on a mattress on the floor, lay a young woman, thin and wasted, who even to my inexperienced eyes looked very sick. The truth of this was of course not known to me at that time, but this was another victim of tuberculosis, so prevalent in those days and an illness which then, more often than not, proved fatal.

At other times I would play with my friends on the Green, a plot of wasteland at the street corner. Ownership of this land had been the subject of dispute for many years so that it was now regarded as common land. Here, goats were tethered to graze and we children played cricket or foot-

A view down Cowley Road in 1917. The church of SS Mary and John is in the background on the left and a milk delivery cart is approaching on the right

'The Home of Compassion'

ball, dug trenches and fought battles, much to the harassment of the poor lady whose house adjoined the Green. The constant battering of balls up against her wall caused the china on her dresser to fall and shatter and the succession of small children tapping on her front door to ask for balls which had bounced into her back garden must have driven her to distraction. But to children, these things were trivial and, though her threats and warnings were heeded for a while, inevitably, high spirits dimmed memory and before long the games were again in full swing.

Opposite the Green, at the junction of Catherine Street with Howard Street, lay a range of stone buildings with blue slate roofs, built in the mid-nineteenth century. Originally intended as a farmhouse, it was said that the high cost of transporting the stone for these buildings, by horse and cart from Bletchingdon, finally bankrupted the builder and the structure was eventually completed as four separate dwellings. However, a Deed of Conveyance relating to this property and dated 29 September 1866 states:

> the four several messuages or dwelling houses and outbuildings erected and built on the said pieces or parcels of land or some part or parts thereof which have been recently converted into one messuage or

range of buildings are now called or commonly known by the name of 'The Home of Compassion'.

This, it is understood, was a home set up by Father Richard Meux Benson, then vicar of Cowley, for the care and shelter of unmarried mothers and must have been in existence for about six years, for a later Conveyance, dated 1872 reads: 'which said "Home of Compassion" has been recently by the said Edward Glanville reconverted into the said four messuages'. The land involved in these Conveyances is described as being 'off the Oxford–Henley Turnpike road'.

Of this block of four dwellings the double-fronted corner house was, in the 1920s, sometimes the venue for prayer meetings presided over by a gentleman who styled himself 'Bishop of Mercia', though by whose authority is not known. His home, complete with private chapel, was in north Oxford, but it was his custom to rent rooms of private houses (he had another in Charles Street, St Ebbe's) where he periodically held services for the benefit of local residents and in which practice he would enlist the aid of local boys as servers. They, with the disrespect of youth, referred to him as Bungy. These functions were poorly attended; sometimes the lady of the house was the sole worshipper and she, at the insistence of the 'Bishop', always put on hat and coat before entering her own front room where the altar was set out but, undaunted, he would celebrate the entire service of Mass as though to a full congregation. The denomination of his calling was obscure, but his activities were certainly frowned upon by the clergy of the parish of Cowley St John.

In the front room window of this same house stood a large glass jar of water covered with a small cloth, in which small particles of yeast bubbled, rose and fell at intervals. Periodically this mixture was fed with brown sugar, the yeast particles split so multiplying and, after about two weeks, the whole bubbling mass was strained, bottled and left to mature. The result was a clear golden liquid known as 'bee wine' and was very potent. Many window sills in the district displayed evidence of this latest craze, believed to have started just after the 1914–18 war, but, after some months, rumour said it was injurious to health and the window jars quickly disappeared.

Directly opposite our house lived an old lady to whom I would often be sent with eggs which she had ordered. Short, and savagely corseted, her head a halo of white fluff, she was very kind and invited me in to her house, but I always felt rather afraid of her for her house was very dark with a smell of mould. On reflection, this was probably because every available nook and cranny was filled with ferns and pot plants of many varieties on which she obviously lavished much care, but I always felt myself to be in a gloomy mysterious cavern and was relieved to be let out into the sunshine again.

Most of our neighbours were hardworking people, not above a little gossip, but always ready to help in times of trouble. The men were mostly craftsmen of one kind or another: carpenters, builders, decorators, plumbers and their womenfolk prided themselves on their skill and their ability to manage. Of course there were problem families; some with a permanent chip on their shoulders; others who revelled in verbal exchanges; and those who simply gave up under the constant worry of coping with life. For the young and fit life was good, but the old or sick depended to a great extent on their families, neighbours, or, failing these, the Poor Law institution in Cowley Road. (During the 1914–18 war this establishment had been taken over for use as a military hospital, and local sick or poor people had been transferred to Headington, Woodstock or Chipping Norton.)

In Catherine Street, near its junction with Magdalen Road lay a row of terraced houses which, in contrast to those opposite, had no front gardens. Front doors opened directly on to the pavement and access to the rear of the premises was gained through an alley in the centre of the block. Here poverty and the will to struggle on survived side by side, sometimes in harmony, sometimes in discord. Some houses were clean, others were not; from the curtainless, downstair window of one such house peered the drawn face, framed by matted hair, of an old lady. Who she was I do not know; if anyone cared for her I do not know; whenever I passed her window she was there, just gazing out, and this was so for many, many weeks. Eventually, I heard that she had knocked over a candle, setting light to her bedclothes, and was burned to death.

We had another neighbour who seemed to find us, and the noise we made, a source of great irritation. She lived in a small terraced house overlooking the Green and appeared to wait, concealed behind her lace curtains, until the wicket had been hammered in or the goal-post jackets laid in place, then she would sail out to her front gate gesticulating angrily: 'Be off, go and play somewhere else!'

It must be admitted that there was 'somewhere else'. At the bottom of the street lay the recreation ground known to local children as the 'rec.'. This playground was bordered on its south-western side by a wide ditch and stream which afforded many energetic hours of ditch jumping and climbing trees. The north-eastern boundary lay along the main road to Cowley, at that time flanked by hedges, in the south-east more hedges, and on the north-west boundary, allotments.

Swings and a maypole were provided, and cared for by groundsman Mr Lardner, an ex-military man and strict disciplinarian, who sat in a little hut on the north-west side. Smartly dressed and in good time every morning, he would be at his post hanging the swings by chains and fastening the maypole handles. With equal diligence he would dismantle this equipment at

Cowley recreation ground, photographed in 1901 by the renowned photographer Henry Taunt whose house 'Rivera' is in the background. The sheep were used to keep the grass short

night and lock it away, but entrance to the ground was still possible by means of white kissing-gates on the north-east and south-west boundaries. Inevitably, at night, the ground became a haunt for courting couples rather than children.

Occasionally Mr Lardner would be helped in his task by the advent of our local policeman, who made it his business to look in at the rec. A very corpulent character was Bobby King, a stalwart sidesman at St Alban's church and fearfully respected by most of us. To be discovered in some misdemeanour by his stentorian cry of 'Oy!', or to find his bulky figure blocking the way, was enough to send most of us scuttling home. Encountering a

'Swings and a maypole were provided...'

gang of boys with bulging jerseys and instantly diagnosing apple scrumping, he would transfix them with a glare and demand names. These being supplied, he would administer a sharp cuff round the head and follow this with a visit to their parents. This treatment was usually sufficient for the cause of order and the hours spent on the rec. were generally peaceful and idyllic.

Many were the picnics held there on hot Saturday afternoons, with sticky buns and 'marble' bottles of lemonade, which, after lying in the hot sun for some time became unpleasantly tepid. It was a common sight to see children on the swings suspended upside down with legs curled around the seat, or hanging by one hand from a maypole handle, resulting in nothing worse than a knee or an elbow grazed by the asphalt. Around the swings the grass was coarse and kept under some control by sheep which grazed under the eye of a shepherd who lived nearby. He was, as one imagines a shepherd, ruddy complexioned, sturdy and carried a thumbstick.

Once a year the rec. was closed to the public, its gates chained and padlocked, in order that a right of way might not be established.

# CHAPTER THREE

# WORK AND THE LACK OF IT

To the right of the rec. entrance from Howard Street two large black iron gates gave access to the allotments. Land such as this, rented out in sections each about ten pole in size, was greatly sought after and in 1920 about three hundred acres of land in Oxford were under allotment. Many fruitful hours work were spent here by allottees, and for my friends and me it was just another playground. On Good Friday it was traditional to help father plant potatoes, breaking off for elevenses, hot cross buns and lemonade, partaken in the little ramshackle hut erected on his plot for storage of tools etc. I took great pride in this little hut, sweeping it out and tidying up as I had seen mother do at home, but when I proposed hanging curtains over its one small grimy window, father laughed and Norman scornfully dismissed the idea as sissy. These huts were very primitive constructions, built with odd planks and corrugated iron, but here and there could be seen old hansom cab bodies adapted for this purpose. Each plot was separated from its neighbour by a grassy path which led to one of the main roads dividing the expanse and along which it was possible to ride a bicycle or scooter in complete freedom and, if one was unlucky enough to fall off, there was always available the soft cushion of a marrow bed or compost heap.

Come the autumn and the concrete surface stretching from our back door to the lawn was covered with the harvest of our labours: King Edward and Arran Pilot potatoes were spread out on old sacks to dry off before storage and father would suspend several pieces of rope, knotted at one end, from a cross bar, then mother and I would sit stringing the onions. Starting at the lower knotted end, the stem of each onion was twisted twice around the rope so that each beautiful, shiny ball of delicate amber and green lay gently on its predecessor, and the whole swinging cluster was then hung in an outhouse. Old coarse runner beans were picked from the now shrivelling

Lye Hill, Cowley. The path leads up to what is now the Southfield golf course

plants and the big purple, black-spotted beans shelled into a tin to be stored as next year's seed. So we provided for the winter.

It was possible to walk through a gate at the bottom of our garden direct-ly onto our plot, for the allotments ran along behind the house where I lived, meeting the country road to Iffley, edged on their far side by the Withy brook which in 1922 was a boundary of Oxford.

The Withy, so far as we could trace, sprang from Lye Hill near the Cowley Marsh, an open area of land used for recreational purposes. It sparkled through narrow fissures in the hillside, past sedge grass and meadowsweet, tumbling finally into the wide ditch which skirted the Marsh, flowing underneath the main road to Cowley and from then on it became a brook coursing through clusters of willow herb and nettles along-side the allotments. From here it wandered beneath Iffley Road and across

The view from Henry Taunt's house looking towards Crescent Road across Cowley Marsh in 1914. Oxford Road is on the right. The Cowley Road bus garage now occupies this site

fields to join the Thames quite near to the free ferry; but it was the stretch of this waterway bordering the allotments which attracted most of our attention.

In places its banks were bordered on both sides by willow trees whose branches met and entwined over the water, so forming a mysterious green-shaded tunnel: a challenge for the venturesome where the water flowed darkly and the only noise to be heard was the rustle of leaves and the occasional plop of a water rat. The brook was crossed officially in two places by flat concrete bridges, but we scorned these, preferring to cross by strategically placed stepping-stones or to leap from one bank to the other. The banks were sandy and crumbling with tufty grass footholds, so that yellow-stained hands and knees were a common sight, and if misjudgement resulted in a bootful of water, who cared? On the far side of the brook surrounded by tall trees lay a buttercup field and here, discarded boots and socks were spread out to dry in the sun while we ran barefoot in the lush green grass.

But life was not all play: each Saturday morning I was expected to help mother in the house before going out with my friends. These tasks were not performed very graciously or even thoroughly at first but, having been called back a few times to do the job properly, I learned that I might as well get it right first time; so the duster was poked into all corners of the stairs and banisters and the lavatory seat was well polished. Cleaning generally was very hard work at this time. Cutlery was mostly of steel and needed to be cleaned of stains after every meal on a knife-board spread with bath-brick. There were, of course, no vacuum cleaners as we know them today, just mops and brooms, and polish was often made at home from a mixture of melted beeswax and turpentine. Mother cleaned the windows with a chamois leather soaked in a solution of paraffin and water and to perform this operation she would raise the lower window sash and sit out on the sill, her back to the roadway. Even the pavements outside the houses were not neglected, each housewife sweeping the section fronting her house, and this was done daily.

About twice a year it was necessary to have the chimney swept and how we all hated the chaos caused by this necessity. Having stripped the room of movable furniture and swathed the rest in dustsheets the previous night, mother rose early to admit the sweep. He was a little man, black from head to toe and, peeping from my bedroom window watching his arrival at about 6 a.m. on a bicycle with box carrier containing the brushes and rods of his trade, I used to wonder why he ever chose such an unpleasant occupation. Probably he was one of the many men employed in the building trade who were thrown out of work during frosty winter months and were obliged, by their own initiative, to devise another means of subsistence. Chimney sweeping, house decorating and repair jobs were eagerly sought, but these were few and far between, so many relied on casual labour on the roads and their women-folk on laundry work or sewing to see them through a difficult period.

There were some vacancies advertised for women: 'Working cook-housekeeper wanted. Wages £40 p.a. Parlourmaids £30 p.a.' but for men the situations vacant were mostly agricultural, for shepherds, cowmen, carters and thatchers.

Accommodation was sometimes included with these jobs; otherwise houses were available around £395, cottages for £270, and even a pig and poultry farm of twelve acres, plus a seven-roomed twelve-year-old house, with water over the sink, farm buildings and piggeries, freehold for £1,000.

But purchase of property was beyond the reach of many people, most of whom lived in rented houses and concerned themselves with finding a job and keeping it. So desperate were conditions that one of our neighbours, unable to find work locally but being offered employment in London, accepted gratefully and pedalled back and forth to his home at weekends on a push-bike.

The situation was further aggravated by a depression in the Welsh mining industry (culminating in the Pit Strike of 1926, when many collieries closed, causing great hardship among the Welsh people). Miners were leaving their homeland in the search for work and many came to Oxford, some by train while others, unable to spare a pound note for the train fare, formed themselves into groups and made the journey on foot. This took about two weeks with stops at workhouses on the way for a night's lodging, for which hospitality they paid the following morning by executing certain jobs set by the workhouse taskmaster.

In Oxford most were successful in obtaining employment at the Morris motor works then expanding at Cowley. There were, of course, difficulties with accommodation: those who had some money found lodging in local houses; some slept under hedges; some, through the kindness of Mr R. Johnson, lived in caravans parked in a field opposite the works where a coffeestall was provided and well patronized; but others spent many months under canvas in the fields of a nearby farm. When holidays allowed, these men returned to their beloved valleys and one such occasion is vividly remembered by a relative who was at that time a young man working away from Oxford:

> I remember coming home for Christmas that year and my father met me at the station on Christmas Eve. He was very impressed by the platform being crowded with Welshmen going home for Christmas

Johnson's Field, Cowley, with temporary accommodation for workers at the motor works in the 1930s

Morris employees leaving the Cowley works in 1923

they were all singing in the usual Welsh custom. Passengers in trains going through were leaning out of the carriage windows to get a glimpse of the singers.

Despite this natural desire to return home, many men eventually settled in Oxford and brought their families here, away from the black mountains of despair.

We were fortunate in that my father who had been trained as a blacksmith working in a small forge in Dawson Street was also skilled in wrought-iron work and general metal work and, when horse transport began to diminish, he trained also as a plumber. To have a second string to one's fiddle in those days was a great advantage, so maybe the chimney sweep was quite happy in his dirty job and my sympathy misplaced.

Back in bed, for mother had warned me to keep out of the way, I would listen to the rods thrusting the brush up the chimney past my bedroom fireplace and out into the open sky, then rattling down again; and that horrible job was over for another six months.

When mother finally called me, breakfast would be ready and I came down to a room now clean, the floor washed over and the furniture polished, but it did not look like home again until the many pictures had been washed and replaced on the walls. At this time, the manufacturers of Pears soap issued large-size copy engravings depicting romantic or Biblical subjects and these were collected, framed and hung on walls. My home was no exception and I was particularly fond of 'Wake up, it's Christmas morning', 'The soldier's return', and 'Moses in the bulrushes'.

Breakfast on these mornings had to be eaten in the kitchen: for father eggs and bacon, but we preferred bread with lard, sugar or dripping. Norman and Joyce had good appetites, but I was rather finicky and felt I could have existed quite happily on bread and butter, though I can recall being hoisted on father's knee and fed with 'soldiers' of fried bread and bacon which I ate with relish.

It was customary to have four meals a day at home. Dinner was at midday, with a meat course and always a pudding such as roly-poly suet, boiled apple pudding or steamed jam sponge. The Sunday roast was traditionally beef with Yorkshire pudding, but in the week the meat course consisted mainly of such things as heart, liver, sausages and boiled sheep's head with dumplings. I ate this latter meal sparingly; I could never quite adjust my taste to the red meat scraped from that grinning skull or meet the reproachful look which seemed to emanate from its empty eye sockets; neither would my gorge accept the black puddings, chitterlings and pigs' trotters so enjoyed by my father. Tea was a fairly light meal of bread and butter with cake, and for supper a meat meal for father but cereals and milk puddings for us.

A great deal of work was involved in the preparation of food. Always on the range stood a large iron pot, the stockpot, into which went vegetables, bacon rind, scraps of meat to be cooked down and used for gravy or soup. Stale bread was dried and browned in the oven, then rolled into breadcrumbs, and the water in which bacon had been boiled was left to cool and the fat skimmed from its surface. We always had in our larder a big bowl of brown dripping taken from underneath the Sunday joint and this was delicious on toast or bread. Most of our food was home cooked: flour cost 9d. a pound, margarine 1s. a pound, and a pound of tea was 1s. 10d.; limited refrigeration was available for those who could afford to invest in an ice chest.

A typical full-course luncheon at one of the large restaurants in Oxford included soup or fish, a joint and vegetables, sweet, cheese, rolls and coffee and cost around 2s. 3d., but people of our acquaintance rarely ate out, restaurants were for the well-to-do and there was less demand for pub meals or small cafés than is the case today. Many working people and schoolchildren preferred to take sandwiches for their midday meal; though some senior schools supplied dinners for pupils, often prepared by the cookery class, but from the infant school I attended we were collected by parents and ate our meal at home.

# CHAPTER FOUR

# LEARNING AND LIVING

SS Mary and John Infants' School, built 1902, was a pleasant red-brick building which lay behind high iron railings in Hertford Street, and it was here, at the age of four years, that my formal education commenced. My first impression on entering the cloakroom was of many equally bewildered infants, rows of pegs and shoe-bags. The walls of this dimly lit enclosure were tiled, and in winter they almost permanently streamed with condensation.

The headmistress was Miss Rogers whom we called 'the Governess', and she sat behind a raised square desk on which reposed a big brass bell. Clad always in an immaculate white apron, she appeared outwardly very stern but was, in reality, a very human and understanding lady. The babies' class was supervised by an adult teacher, Miss Davies, and her assistant 'teacher Winnie'. Poor teacher Winnie, she it was who broke up the fights, collected the named packets of lunch in a huge red bag which smelt of bread and butter, and she who washed out the wet pants. The classroom was large but the windows were set high in the wall so that no small mind should be distracted from work by the world outside. There was a sandpit and a rocking-horse and my introduction to the world of mathematics was by means of a bead frame and coloured sticks. For one hour during the afternoon the little ones were allowed to sleep, but for the more active there were games or modelling with sticky grey clay. Twice a day we were released into the playground, an asphalt area bounded at one end by a grass plot with a few trees which was forbidden territory, and behind the school, but apart from the main building, stood a row of lavatories.

The floor of the main hall was covered with chalk crosses and minus marks on which each child stood so that morning assembly appeared quite an orderly affair. As I progressed through the school I found the discipline became more strict: I was expected to sit up straight in the two-seater desk with arms folded behind my back and to my cost, found that any pupil who drooped, and oh it was so easy on a hot day, was brought sharply upright by a tap on the knuckles from a ruler. I learned to move from class to class quietly and at a walking pace, governed by a wooden instrument used by the teacher and called a 'clicker'. This emitted a rhythmic beat so that one marched in time; again, any defaulter received a quick tap on the head.

Children from the Poor Law school at Cowley shared our schooling. This institution catered for about 140 boys and girls between the ages of three and fifteen: orphaned, deserted, or perhaps simply in need of care which their parents for some reason were unable to provide. The children were well disciplined and despite their underprivileged beginnings and the separation from their parents, often did well in later life. Girls were usually sent into service and the boys to join the Army or Navy, to do farm work or were apprenticed to a trade. Maybe they fared better than those who, because their parents received 'outdoor relief', escaped the supervision of the Poor Law guardians.

During these years at the infant school we were several times given a day off when the building was needed as a polling station for political elections. There were exciting preliminaries to these events: rival factions formed among the children and fights and skirmishes often ensued. A rhyme chanted with much gusto on these occasions ran:

> Vote, vote, vote for Captain Bourne [the Conservative candidate],
> Knock old Frankie out the way [the Liberal candidate].
> For if Frankie should win,
> He'll do us all in,
> So vote, vote, vote for Captain Bourne.

The supporters of the Liberal candidate would in turn shout their reversed version of this rhyme and the scuffle which followed ended with a few scratched faces and torn clothing.

I was lucky to have an expert needlewoman for a mother and possessed quite an extensive wardrobe, albeit made from old material. At school I wore a white broderie-anglaise pinafore (later coloured pinafores became popular), on the left side of which was pinned a handkerchief; this latter object was compulsory equipment for all pupils. Before morning prayers we were inspected by Miss Rogers and anyone unable to produce a handkerchief was given a piece of paper. Many girls had long hair, mine was short, but we all wore brightly coloured hair-ribbons in cheerful contrast to the boys, many of whom, in the style of the day, had their hair completely shorn except for a tuft in the front, partly for reasons of economy and also because it lessened the likelihood of head lice. This style was known as the 'fourpenny-all-over'.

Several times a year the school was visited by Nurse Button who examined our heads for livestock and kept a look-out for rickets, once a common result of malnutrition; but happily by 1920 this disease was decreasing, though children in callipers were still to be seen. Rife among the children was ringworm, to which I fell victim, much to mother's dismay, for it was a disagreeable infection which necessitated cutting off all my hair until the scalp cleared, and I was obliged to wear a little mob cap until my hair grew again. Children who had not been vaccinated against smallpox at birth were often so treated at this age and, as a warning against rough handling, would wear a red ribbon tied around the affected arm. As I had been vaccinated as a baby I was denied this privilege and the importance it engendered, much to my disappointment.

Sometimes the nurse would be accompanied by the school dentist who arrived with trays of pink cards, each bearing diagrams of upper and lower teeth, crossed or ringed according to attention previously given and was allocated a classroom into which we filed, sick in the stomach, for inspection. If treatment was deemed necessary we were obliged to attend, in the company of an adult, a clinic then held in St Aldate's. I dreaded these visits and was always relieved to step out of that high chair leaving behind the tray of shiny instruments and the bloody spit, to emerge into the open air clutching my crossed-off card and a well-earned copy of *Chick's Own*. Later a clinic was set up in the Cowley Road workhouse which lay at the end of a drive, oddly very short in length on the way in and surrounded by prickly bushes and trees but which, on the return journey, became a long sunlit path through gay flowers and shrubs, and my feet, previously so leaden, now skipped and hopped back to my lessons.

With all this supervision over our health it could surely not have been an Oxford schoolmaster who, on complaining to a mother of the uncleanliness of her son, received the following startling reply: 'Our Johnnie ain't no rose, you larn him, don't smell him!'

I was very happy at this school, but at the age of seven years, being no longer infants, my contemporaries and I were obliged to leave. Normally children progressed from here to the 'Big Boys' (Headmaster: Mr J. Irving) or 'Big Girls' (Headmistress: Miss M. Tidmarsh), both housed in one building next to the infant school, but with separate entrances for either sex. The girls entered from Essex Street to the first floor and the boys from Hertford Street to the ground floor.

The repair and upkeep of these three schools was the financial responsibility of the church and appeals for money were therefore often to be found in the parish magazine.

In May 1920: 'We have to asphalt the playground of our boys' school, the estimate is £150'. To be followed in October 1920 by the depressing news: 'The asphalting of the school playground will cost about double what we expected. So far I have received an anonymous gift of ten shillings!'

By February 1925 the situation had apparently deteriorated: 'we are in trouble about the schools which have been partially condemned'. But, somehow, the money from parishioners and various funds must have materialized: 'During the past three years the exteriors of both schools have been re-painted involving an expenditure of approximately £150 on these two items alone.'

Parents were, however, allowed some choice in the matter of schools and I was sent to 'Sister Alice's', an establishment for girls only, staffed by both nuns and lay teachers. Originally under the headship of Sister Alice, a small but capable lady, pupils had paid sixpence a week for the privilege of attending this school, plus a few pence extra for specialized subjects such as French, but in 1924 Miss Vincent was headmistress and there was no charge for attendance. Members of the Society of St John the Evangelist often visited the school to give religious instruction; among these were Father Sedding and Father Tovey, both of whom later left England to become missionaries. Discipline here was strict with a view to turning out young ladies. Here I was taught to sit properly and conduct myself in a seemly manner, also to be punctual! I had become the despair of the headmistress because, despite leaving home in good time, I constantly arrived at school after classes had started, and to correct this I was put in the care of a prefect who had orders to call for me every morning and bring me to school. This so shamed me, for I was fearful my parents might find out, that I promised the prefect to meet round the corner out of sight of home and in good time for school. It says much for the psychology of the headmistress that there were no more late mornings.

The school was divided into four houses named after heroic women: St Frideswide, Joan of Arc, Florence Nightingale, and I was in Grace Darling's house. There was great competition between the houses in connection with sports or examinations and generally it was a very successful school and produced good results. Though I fared pretty well in most subjects, I found arithmetic particularly difficult. Many the tears I shed in my efforts to calculate nineteen yards of red ribbon at 1s. 11¾d. a yard, or to work out the vagaries of leaking baths and dripping taps, and it was not until I reached secondary school that I emerged from the fog of mathematical confusion and began to enjoy the subject. At the age of ten or eleven all pupils sat for the scholarship, after which the successful candidates went on to a higher grade school and the remainder to the 'Big Girls' in Essex Street.

We three children suffered the usual childish ailments during these early years: measles, croup, mumps, chicken-pox and whooping-cough, for the only immunization then generally available was for smallpox. Fortunately, diphtheria was becoming less common: Norman had suffered this dangerous malady when only about twelve months old, a crisis with which my mother had coped alone, for at that time my father was serving in France during the First World War.

Another trial during those war years, though much less serious was Bob, a black mongrel dog. Originally bought by father as company and protection for mother while he was away in France Bob was, instead, a troublemaker. Mother was constantly apologizing for his wild fighting and other misdemeanours until, faced one day with a demand for recompense from the irate owner of a dead chicken, she decided a new home would have to be found for Bob and he was passed on to one of father's many acquaintances, a gentleman more able to cope with a boisterous animal.

An illness frequently occurring among children was scarlet fever. When this was diagnosed in Norman and Joyce they were both immediately taken away in the 'fever cart' to an isolation hospital in Abingdon Road and their rooms fumigated. The shock of their departure, swathed in blankets and in the arms of a crisply efficient nurse, really frightened me and gave me nightmares. I was dosed by a well-meaning neighbour with brimstone and treacle, a ghastly mixture, but maybe it helped for I remained free of the disease. Norman and Joyce were kept in quarantine for a few weeks and mother and father were allowed to visit, though they were obliged to stand at a window outside the hospital ward, while I was not allowed that far but was left at the porter's lodge to await their return. Joyce was barely two years old, but true to the moral code of those days she was separated from Norman and put into the female ward. However, she protested so noisily and at such length that the staff were only too glad to bend the rules and she was allowed to have her bed next to Norman in the male ward, where she ruled like a queen.

A neighbour who was very kind and a comfort to my mother at this time was Mrs Chaundy who lived opposite. With no family of her own, each Christmas she gave parties for children from the street, with balloons and oranges as parting gifts, and was often to be seen riding around the streets on an old bicycle and perched on a basket strapped to the rear carrier rode her pet jackdaw. One room of her house had black painted walls and ceiling, for her husband was a photographer employed by the Ashmolean Museum and this was his studio. He was much in demand locally for weddings or when new babies arrived.

Babies were mostly born at home in those days under the supervision of visiting midwives, of whom Nurse Stack was an admirable example, and minor ailments were often self-treated at home with a 'bottle from the chemist'. It was also possible to buy proprietary brands of medicine from most general stores: Parrish's food and cod liver oil for pale children, syrup of figs for stubborn children and ipecacuanha wine or paregoric for troublesome coughs; but for stronger treatment people contributed to the Cutler

Marston Street in the 1930s showing the dispensary (left) to which the author's father paid a subscription for medical treatment in the event of family illness

Boulter Provident Dispensary (Estd. 1885) in Marston Street. This cost a few pence per family per week, but included the attention of a doctor, prescribed medicines, and provided a valuable service. One entered the dispensary through double glass doors leading to a large waiting-room filled with long benches on which patients sat until summoned into the surgery at the end of a long, dark passage by the sharp 'ting' of a bell. During this wait people would converse in low hushed voices and their conversation, as far as I could make out, was always of illness, of how the doctor had 'never seen anything like it', accompanied by nods and grimaces, intending, no doubt, to convey that their suffering was unique. I was always glad when our turn came to venture down that dim passageway to where Dr Kewley awaited us. Rather abrupt in manner, but a very kind and devoted doctor, he was widely respected. These trips to the dispensary usually took the entire morning, so dinner was a casual affair and our pudding was often a cake procured from Jackson's bakery in Hurst Street, on the way home.

In addition to this medical care, many families paid a weekly contribution of a few pence to the Radcliffe Infirmary, and for this one received full hospital treatment. In later years, the contribution was paid at one's place of work and deducted from the wage packet.

Other assistance was obtained from provident clubs, slate clubs organized by public houses providing sick benefit for their members or by contributing to a Friendly Society, such as the Independent Order of Oddfellows to which my father belonged. This society, in the event of illness or the incapacity of the breadwinner, provided immediate medical attendance, financial assistance to the tune of a few shillings a week, and death benefit. A week off work, whatever the reason, meant no pay and so it naturally followed that holidays for adults were very infrequent. I was ten years old before my parents could afford to take us for a week to the seaside. Nevertheless, there were bank holidays to be anticipated and planned for, and Ascension Day, Empire Day and May Day were great events in our calendar.

# CHAPTER FIVE

# MAY DAY

Annually, on the morning of 1 May, a simple but impressive ceremony takes place from the top of Magdalen College tower, an edifice which took fourteen years to build and was completed in 1506. There are several schools of thought as to the origin of this ceremony: some hold that it is a survivor of the inauguration celebrations on the completion of the building; others that it originated at the requiem mass for Henry VII; and again, that it might be of greater antiquity, being a relic of earlier worship of the sun.

However this might be, the occurrence is held in great regard by Oxonians and attracts visitors from far and near. Originally held at 5 a.m., the time was changed somewhere around the end of the eighteenth century and in the 1920s, the appointed hour was 6 a.m. From 5.30 a.m. onwards, shadowy figures on foot, both young and old, many wheeling bicycles, loomed out of the early morning mist and gathered on the big stone bridge at the foot of the tower until the roadway was completely blocked. The younger children, wearing flower-decorated hats, came with hoops and staves gaily decorated with wild flowers: primroses, cowslips, bluebells; and sitting against the parapet of the bridge displayed these works of floral art for all to see, inviting expressions of appreciation in a flower-decked collection box.

Above the hubbub of chatter, laughter and shouted greeting rang out the discordant blast of may-horns, vigorously blown by the rowdier element, but the atmosphere was good-humoured and expectant.

As the hour of six approached faces were raised to the top of the tower which was by now packed with members of the Magdalen College Chapel choir attired in white surplices and, as if by command (though no order was given), a great hush fell upon the crowd and in that still, cool air nothing but the occasional twitter of birds could be heard and on the hour, to the straining ears below, floated the faint, sweet sound of the singing of the Latin *Hymnus Eucharisticus*:

May Day on Magdalen Tower

*Te Deum Patrem colimus*
*Te laudibus prosequimor*
*Qui corpus cibo reficis*
*Coelesti mentem gratia.*

The crowd below remained silent, still, savouring the serenity of the moment. For this they had left their warm beds and shaken sleepy-eyed children into consciousness; for these few moments, to be remembered always, the world was at peace.

> If you wander down the High sir,
> You'll round the bend to spy
> The tower of Magdalen College
> Framed against the sky.
> Alongside, a wide stone bridge
> The meandering Cherwell spans.
> Folk gather there on May morning,
> Children with flower garlands.
> And Morris dancers all in white
> With bells below the knee,
> In the street perform their dance

Of great antiquity.
At six o'clock the voices hush,
All eyes are raised on high.
From tower top a choir sings,
The sound comes as a sigh
Borne on the cold crisp air
To delight the ear below,
A surplice flutters now and then
That's all there is to show.
But that's a treasured memory sir,
And none can take from me,
The fragrance of that morning
And the river's song of glee.

The peace was for a few minutes only; no sooner had the last notes died away, fading into the great expanse of lightening sky, than the throng came to life! With cheering and blowing of may-horns, they flocked to the balustrade of the bridge, fighting for vantage points and gazing expectantly at the river below. They were not to be disappointed: the many punts, mostly occupied by undergraduates and their lady friends, which, during the singing had been quietly moored to the bank, now moved into mid-stream and the fun began. Egged on by cheers from the spectators, these

Magdalen Bridge, Oxford, in the 1930s

33

young men leapt gaily from boat to boat, resulting in the inevitable immersion of many of the participants. The onlookers, some hanging perilously over the balustrade of the bridge, jeered and encouraged this sport and offered nothing but laughter to the bedraggled objects who were dragged or towed ashore by their companions.

When this diversion palled, the crowd thronged before Queen's College or other chosen spots where the Morris dancers performed. Their dances have been executed in rural England at fairs or on village greens for centuries and there is little doubt that they were in existence, in various forms, in pagan times and were then religious ceremonial dances intended to invoke fertility. The groups of dancers, dressed in white, wore bell pads below the knee which then merely accentuated the rhythm of the music but may well have been once intended to scare off evil spirits; this may also have been the reason for the waving of handkerchiefs and the clashing of sticks. For perhaps the previous one hundred years Headington Quarry had been well known for this activity and their dancing of Headington Morris Reel, Bean Setting, Rigs of Marlow and other dances was frequently accompanied by the concertina playing of that Morris stalwart, William Kimber. Sometimes a violin provided the necessary music, but the rhythm and melody were infectious and matched the mood of the May morning revellers.

Another May Day pastime – Jack in the Green – unfortunately died out within the first few years of the twentieth century. Enacted by the chimney sweeps of the town and carried on in Oxford by the Hathaway family, the performers boasted such intriguing names as Fiddler, Shovel and Scraper, Poker, Money-box and Jack in the Green. Around a green sugar-loaf structure of wicker-work covered with leaves and laurel with flowers between, Jack in the Green reeled around one way, the other dancers moved in the reverse direction, clanging poker, shovel, pot and ladle as they cavorted to the strains of a squeaky violin.

After the dancing, the more energetic of the onlookers set out on the ramble which was an accepted part of May Day morning; or groups of cyclists would pedal their way to Kidlington or Dorchester where it was known that early morning breakfast was available; but we usually took our bicycles and rode to the Baldons, a collection of hamlets lying beyond Nuneham Courtenay to the east of Oxford:

> Marsh Baldon, Toot Baldon
> Baldon on the Green.
> Big Baldon, Little Baldon,
> Baldon in between.

Both Norman and I possessed bicycles, the result of weeks of careful assembly by father: a frame here, wheels there, a few new parts and a pot of black paint. The frame of Norman's cycle was somewhat large for him at first but this was overcome by fitting wooden blocks to the pedals. It was not until I was working and able to save for myself that I had a brand-new bicycle; what concentration went into the perusal of those glossy catalogues before finally setting off with father to buy a new Raleigh cycle costing £6.10.0d!

(It is interesting to note that in a booklet issued for the Oxfordshire Constabulary Centenary 1857–1957, the following statement appears: 'In October 1894 the first official bicycle was bought. It cost £15!')

The narrow country road threaded past the village green: a cool, green carpet in the morning light, its centre smooth-shaven for the convenience of sportsmen and its shaggy fringes dotted with dandelion-gold. Along one border the proud elm stood out against the skyline and a row of pollard willows gave us a clenched fist salute. Unobtrusively encircling the whole expanse were the roofs of Dutch barns and houses, some of warm brick and timber construction, others of stone and thatch. Their occupants were astir by now, doors and windows opened to admit the glory of the morning; noise came from the farmyards, and the milkman waved cheerily to us as we sped past. The clatter of his churns in the cart had brought forth his customers with jugs to be filled and, while he was so engaged, his brown horse cropped the juicy grass of the verges contentedly.

Further on, the road became shaded and wooded and here we would dismount, laying our bicycles on the grassy bank so that I might pick violets or the bright-eyed celandine, and father, seated on a tree-stump green with lichen and sprouting fungi, might smoke a Woodbine.

> A place where I can find sweet violets
> Dampened with morning dew,
> Which shyly bloom in sheltered spot,s
> Nearby, the primrose too.
> There I can see the new fern fronds,
> Of tan and palest green,
> Curling upwards gracefully,
> Determined to be seen.
> I can stain my hands with soft leaf mould,
> Or juice from the bluebell frail.
> I can powder my nose with the pollen which blows
> From the catkin's yellow tail.

By now the sun would be brightening in the blue sky, filtering through the overhanging trees to dapple the roadway before us and we would

May Day celebrations outside the parish school in Iffley in 1906

breathe the cool sweetness of air not yet subjected to the heat of day. Just beyond these lanes lay the fields of Garsington where cowslips grew, but by then it was time to return home, so we pedalled from this peaceful spot out on to the main road leading to Cowley and the Morris works. Along this road, in a field to our left, lay a small building standing in isolation. It was approached through a white gate at the roadside giving access to a long track and on the gate was fixed a small notice board 'Smallpox Hospital'. Each time I passed this little gate I would hold my breath for fear of breathing in a germ, though the place looked deserted and the air may well have been less polluted than the industrial area through which we later passed on our way home, rosy-cheeked and with large appetites for breakfast.

May Day was also an eagerly anticipated event in local schools, notably Iffley, where a queen was elected by private ballot from girls attending the village school and, by a similar procedure, the pupils would also elect a king. Girls in their best white dresses and boys in Sunday suits would process to church in the wake of the king and queen and maids of honour wearing flowers in their hair. At that time there were many snakesheads growing in the riverside fields and these, together with cowslips and other wild flowers gathered early on May Day morning, were deftly formed into gay garlands, though the May Queen was usually presented with a bouquet of lilies. After a short service the children walked to the Rectory and other local houses at which they sang songs and rattled their collecting boxes before returning to the school for tea.

> The summer days are coming, the blossom decks the bough,
> The bees are gaily humming and birds are singing now.
> We have our May-day garment, we've crowned our May-day Queen,
> With a coronal of roses set in leaves of brightest green.

In Headington Quarry children assembled in the schoolroom; the girls dressed in pink frocks and white aprons, the boys in smocks, and very small girls in white with garlands round their heads. The May Queen, elected by the scholars from among the older girls, had six attendants and a page bearing a floral crown on a cushion. Before the maypole the queen was crowned and presented with a bouquet after which the dancing began. Dances such as 'Black Meg', 'The Muffin Man' and 'The Prince has come a-riding', were followed by 'open tent' plaiting of the maypole – a very effective sight.

A secret ballot was also organized to choose the queen for celebrations at East Oxford school, and as a memento she was presented with a locket and chain. A platform was erected in the playground and gaily decorated, and from this elevated position the queen reigned over the festivities. There were country dances, including maypole dancing and boys performed traditional Morris dances before an audience of parents and friends.

The 'Big Boys' and 'Big Girls' also celebrated the crowning of a May Queen and the revels took place in the gardens of St John's Home, near to the schools. The pattern was much the same, folk dancing and singing by white-clad children, watched by their proud parents, teaching staff and parishioners of SS Mary and John.

CHAPTER SIX

# THE GENERAL STRIKE

In 1926 the glory of May Day was quickly overtaken by the incidence of the General Strike, the shadow of which hung menacingly over the preceding years. In April a government subsidy to the mining industry ceased and the miners, who were being asked to work longer hours for less pay refused and stopped work altogether. A national strike was called by the General Council of the Trades Union Congress, with the authority of the unions, in support of the miners whose slogan was:

Not a penny off the pay,
Not a minute on the day

and on 4 May, industrial works throughout the country responded by ceasing work and many vital services were affected. London was described as 'strangely still' and one newspaper commented: 'Buses stood like silent toys in their depots', and: 'In the docks only seagulls and wharf rats moved – not a winch creaked'.

There was a rush of volunteers to maintain essential services and in Oxford residents and undergraduates enrolled as special constables or drove lorries in convoys to the docks to collect food. There were enthusiastic scenes outside the general post office in St Aldate's when several hundred undergraduates, conspicuous in their plus-fours and brightly coloured pullovers left, in whatever transport could be commandeered by the police, for Hull and Southampton to work as dockers. A gleaming new limousine, making its way through Oxford, was stopped by a constable:

'Where to?' he asked of the driver.

'Scarborough' was the reply, 'to deliver this new car'.

'Right, just the man we want' said the constable and calling to a group of three undergraduates:

'Hi, you three, jump up here', and to the startled driver:

'Drop these men at Hull'. And so it was all day long.

But the volunteers were not welcomed at their destination and were attacked by resentful mobs, kicked and spat upon, though more often than not these attacks were made by rowdies and not genuine strikers. When the strike ended the following notice was found in a meat van at the Great Western Railway station:

Southampton Docks.
Docks for dockies. College for baggies!
Don't trespass again, please.

The derivation of 'baggies' as a new name for the undergraduates was obvious.

Generally Oxford remained calm and saw little of the violence experienced in London or Hull. Morris Motors continued working, as did the gas company, but local printers, bricklayers and plasterers ceased work, though carpenters, painters and labourers did not, which inevitably led to disruption in the building trade and many men were laid off because of shortage of supplies.

On the railway platforms large piles of luggage stood with milk cans and a few hopeful passengers. There were a few trains running, driven by volunteers, no doubt realizing a childhood ambition! Asked by a passenger what he thought of the strike one such enthusiast replied: 'What do I think of it, just this – keep smiling and do what you can.' But despite their efforts the *Oxford Times* stated: 'there was a silence about the station quarter of the city such as characterizes the smallest village'.

Oxford busmen refused to strike and a meeting organized with the intention of forcing them out broke up in confusion when they broke into singing 'Land of Hope and Glory'. They encountered some unpleasantness in their efforts to continue working: there were cries of 'Blackleg' and 'Rotter', but these protests were fairly ineffectual and generally stopped short of the physical violence experienced elsewhere.

Volunteers also maintained some kind of postal service, though the postmaster asked that as few letters as possible be posted and did not accept parcels in view of the difficulty of delivery.

However, Oxford did not escape all the hardship consequent upon such an event. Food was not officially rationed as most traders made their own arrangements to collect supplies from London, but, inevitably, this caused scarcity and increased prices. Shoppers were urged not to panic but the price of salmon reached 3s. 3d. a pound, haddock 1s. 1d. a pound, pigeons cost 1s. 6d. each and rabbits 1s. 9d., and such foods as butter and cheese became scarce and expensive.

There were prayers and appeals in the churches for all to remain calm, quoting the message from Prime Minister Baldwin – 'Keep steady'.

Carfax Tower in Oxford in 1922

Newspaper workers did not strike in Oxford, delivering their papers by car and bicycle, and they and the public wireless stations kept the people informed of events. Daily they were besieged by a public anxious for news. They published appeals for transport: 'Would car owner offer to take schoolgirl to London Bridge for Bognor train, Tuesday or Wednesday?' and advised on the postponement of many social functions: dinners, annual general meetings, competitions and of the cancellation of local football matches by order of the Football Association.

There was a strong spirit evident in the people, who were encouraged: 'Do something. Hanging about and swopping rumours is bad in every way'.

There were divided loyalties: at a London elementary school the whole of the teaching staff was late arriving due to the strike. When the staff did arrive they found the senior boys in command maintaining discipline and keeping the younger children busy with reading. Many of these boys were the sons of men on strike!

By 11 May, it was obvious that the strike was weakening; men were gradually drifting back to work realizing the futility of their action. There was still much sympathy with the miners but general opinion appeared to agree with the Master Printers: 'We wish to make it clear that we retain our sympathy with the miners in their struggle for better wages and working conditions, but we fail to see how the ruin of other industries can bring this about.'

On 12 May, the strike ended. It was, said Mr Baldwin, 'a victory for commonsense'. There were wild scenes of relief and joy in Oxford at the news. Excited crowds thronged Carfax, clamouring for the special editions of local newspapers, so that the vendors found difficulty in satisfying the demand.

The miners alone continued the struggle, asserting: 'Reports show that there is greater solidarity every day in the coalfields', but, six months later, they too accepted the uselessness of further resistance and returned to work.

Though I can clearly recall incidents which occurred prior to 1926, I have no recollection of the General Strike and have been obliged to rely on reports and records of the time. This would appear to confirm the comparative outward calmness of Oxford during this troubled period; but for adults, aware of the underlying tension, this must have been a very worrying time. Stocks of food were carefully conserved and money spent cautiously; all thought of holidays and such luxuries was shelved in the uncertainty of the future.

# CHAPTER SEVEN

# HOLIDAYS AND OUTINGS

It was our good fortune that most summers mother took us to spend several weeks holiday with my aunt Eva, first at Ashorne, later at Lillington, Leamington Spa. Aunt Eva's husband was chauffeur to a wealthy lady whose big shiny car was housed in a garage in the yard of my aunt's cottage, but we were collected from Leamington railway station by pony and trap and soon after arriving at the cottage we children were left to explore the huge garden which lay at the top of a flight of steps opposite the kitchen door. It was a children's paradise: a huge orchard, its trees weighed down with fruit. Bright, rosy Worcesters were ours for the picking, but yellow-mellowing Blenheims, Bramleys and smooth Codlins were left to hang until September or October, though nature had thinned out the crop, shedding the speckled over-abundance into the long grass where it split and shattered, a succulent feast for wasps and ants. It was my delight to walk in this orchard early in the morning, slashing at stinging nettles and dock leaves, my shoes dew soaked, mist in my hair, and breathing the fresh, earthy smell of vegetation. There was a kitchen garden mostly tended by my aunt, for uncle was no gardener, and beyond, over a stile, the green folds of the open fields of Warwickshire.

Later my aunt moved to Lillington to another isolated cottage with an equally rambling garden surrounded by fields where brown and white cows munched contentedly. The house lay in a hollow so that the back gardens rose sharply to the level of the bedroom window-sill and I remember still the enchantment of waking in my room with its sloping ceiling and gazing out at the hazy, mist-hung fields with their promise of exploration. We climbed trees in the orchard, willingly fed the hens, or roamed the quiet lanes in joyous and utter freedom. I have happy memories of those seemingly endless weeks.

Each year, in the company of my cousins, we would produce a theatrical show up on the top field which overlooked the orchard. We built a stage of margarine-boxes and tea-chests and dressed up in whatever clothes we could muster. The most memorable of these was a pierrot show with costumes made from old sheets and decorated with pom-poms of red hollyhock blooms. One year my aunt dressed up as her namesake, substituting fig leaves with large cabbage leaves plucked from the kitchen garden, and with her long auburn hair flowing shinily and freely almost to her waist she posed, amid much laughter, for photographs taken by mother. Later, on a visit to the town, the spool of film was left at a chemist's shop but when, after a few days, the time came to collect the finished prints, neither she nor my mother could pluck up courage to enter the shop; for then developing was carried out on the premises by the chemist. So, preferring to remain anonymous, they sent me alone into the shop with the collection slip.

Sometimes I made perfume from rose petals, or helped my aunt in the kitchen for she was skilled in making dandelion, damson, parsnip and other wines, or ginger pop. We would leave to mature in the pantry a big brown crock full of the mixture, on the surface of which floated slices of lemon and particles of yeast. She also made pickles, chutney, sauces and piccalilli, and it was while making the latter one day, when we were all in the kitchen cutting up cauliflower, onions and other ingredients, a pan of boiling vinegar on the stove, that there descended on us a swarm of wasps. We were taken quite unawares, the first inkling being the angry hum as some zoomed through the open doorway, while their relatives pinged in frustration against the window. With shrieks and yells we downed tools and ran straight out of the kitchen and up the bank, pausing only at the top to look back. We were complete in number except for one, aunt Eva; she alone stood firm and we could see her through the window swatting left and right till at last the wasps, having met their match and being considerably depleted in numbers, disappeared as quickly as they had come.

Like all mother's sisters, aunt Eva was a good cook and made mouthwatering farmhouse cakes. With a wedge of this in one hand and sitting by the open window of the cool parlour through which came the fragrance of sweetpeas, I was sublimely happy and often wished I could stay there for ever. But, of course, we had to return home and it was nice to see father again, for in those early years he was never able to afford time off to come with us. Sometimes, when we pressed him to take a holiday he would say: 'One day I'll take you to the Binsey treacle mines', and then we would laugh, for this was a well-known joke among Oxonians referring to a well in the churchyard at Binsey, west of Oxford. Yet behind this frivolous remark lies a charming story. The word 'treacle' is thought to have derived from the old French word *triacle* corrupted from the Latin *theriaca*, from the Greek word *theriaka*, a pharmaceutical term indicating a medicinal compound in use as an antidote for the bite of wild animals – a healing

Summer activities on the river at Oxford in 1922

substance, and its application to Binsey is explained in the following extract from the Revd Arnold Mallinson's book, *Quinquagesimo Anno:*

The Legend of St Ffrediswyde at St Margaret's Holy Well.
   The legendary story of the foundation of the Church of St Margaret at the Well near Binsey is on this wise. When the most Reverend Princess ffrediswyde, Abbess of Oxford, disdaining the attentions of the enamoured prince of Mercia, Algar, had fled to Thornbury of Binsey, she was pursued there by the Prince who had the temerity to attempt to take hold of her hand and was forthwith smitten blind by a great clap of lightning which flashed forth from a justly wrathful Heaven. A sentiment of sorrow then pierced the heart of the Maiden Princess when she saw her lover's plight and immediately there appeared before

her St Margaret of Antioch with her little dragon and St Catherine of Alexandria with her wheel. Little St Margaret told the saint to strike her Abbatial staff in the ground which when it was done there gushed forth a fount of water. The Princess's Lady Maidens then laved the eyes of luckless Algar with this healing tide and forthwith his sight was given back and seeing the error of his ways he stooped to the ground and kissed the hem of the Princess's robe thereafter returning to Oxenford to lead a better and wiser life.

The holy Princess thereupon built a church in that spot which she dedicated to God in the name of St Margaret.

From that day to this Pilgrims have resorted to this sanctified place in countless numbers and still they come.

We never did go to Binsey but, as a family, we managed many day outings: there were charabanc excursions to Burnham Beeches for 5s., or a steamer trip along the River Thames to Day's Lock with a return ticket costing 4s. 8d., or we would cross the river by ferry boat and walk to the fields just beyond Iffley lock.

The lock, newly constructed in 1923/4, was bordered with neatly trimmed grass and flowerbeds, and nearby stood a square, stone house for the lock-keeper. There were two massive gates at either end of the lock wherein steamers and launches were obliged to wait when travelling downstream until the water in the lock had been reduced to the level of the lower waters beyond, then the gates were opened and all craft proceeded on their way to Sandford. For the return journey upstream, the procedure was reversed. The big lock gates were operated manually, first by the turning of wheels fixed on the narrow decking on top of the gates, then by pressure on two large beams which stretched out over the banks, one on either side of the gates, and controlled their movement. To apply such pressure the lock-keeper, bronzed and smartly dressed in peak cap, white shirt and black trousers, and facing away from the lock, would brace his back against the beam and push with his feet against metal struts set in the ground. He never lacked assistance, for the lock was a fascination for young and old and it was accepted that while he manipulated one side, half a dozen straining eager boys braced themselves against the opposite beam and slowly the gates opened.

Parallel with the lock were the rollers for punts and other small craft, edged by the towpath and a shrubbery. Prior to the construction of the lock this shrubbery had been a large expanse of water known as the Iffley Pool, fed by a lasher just before the entrance to the old lock and a favourite spot with fishermen. Pike were said to abound in its depths and there were tales of one very fine specimen known as the 'Iffley Pike'. Mothers would

The toll-gate at Iffley lock in the 1930s

threaten erring children: 'If you don't behave the Iffley Pike'll get you!' As the fame of this fish increased so did estimates of its size and the lock-keeper, with a twinkle in his eye, would tell open-mouthed children: 'When that old pike comes in my lock, I waits till 'e bangs 'is 'ead on the gates at one end and lashes 'is tail on the other end, then I knows it's time to fill up the lock!'

The meadows which lay beyond the lock were ideal for picnics or fishing with nets and jam jars in the many miniature bays of the indented towpath and this we often did on Saturday afternoons or during the long summer holidays; but a walk on Sunday evening was a more formal occasion.

Then we would set out, Joyce and I walking in front dressed in our best dresses, patent shoes, straw hats and gloves, followed by Norman in a sailor suit wielding a walking-stick and mother, arm-in-arm with father bringing up the rear. The latter also had a walking-stick which was put to good use to prod the back of any child who became too lively on the walk through the streets. Joyce and I would amuse ourselves during this part of the walk by alternately substituting for our Christian names the name of the house we passed, or by playing 'I spy', which distraction kept us reasonably subdued, but on reaching the fields we gave vent to our high spirits. Hats and gloves were deposited with mother and we ran like the wind, chased and fell over the tufty, coarse grass and shouted without fear of correction. Mother would pick a bunch of the small pink-tipped daisies, and sitting on the grass, fashion a long daisy chain which she then twisted into a crown for my hair. I loved these fields and the wild flowers which grew there in profusion: moon daisies, quaking grass, buttercups and clover, sometimes snakesheads, were lovingly gathered in hot little hands, so that by the time we reached home, the flowers were more than ready for the jam jar of water into which they were plunged.

Often these walks took us over the railway bridge at Kennington to The Tandem public house. Pubs then were very much beer-houses, so ladies did not enter but sat at the rough wooden tables and benches in the garden outside and shared lemonade and crisps with the children, but this applied usually only to pubs away from one's home area. My mother never visited the Donnington Arms which was our local, though some women did, but even they mostly collected their beer in a jug and took it home to drink. The Donnington was converted from two cottages and on mounting the steps and entering the off-licence, one found oneself looking down through a pall

The Tandem Inn at Kennington in the 1930s, on the route of walks made by the author at this time

of cigarette smoke on to the packed and noisy bar. Later in the evening came the consequent groups of drunks, or those just silly enough to be a nuisance, wending their raucous way home.

But The Tandem was a pleasant country pub and provided a welcome half-way house on a hot summer evening's walk. It possessed attractive gardens and behind a hedge – Aunt Sally. This was a very old country game in which a wooden shape called the 'dolly' was placed on a flat iron ring which swivelled freely on the top of a pole about three feet high. Standing about thirty feet away, players tossed thick wooden sticks, about eighteen inches long, at the dolly in an attempt to dislodge it. Cheers greeted such an achievement, but if the stick merely hit the support, there were jeering cries of 'iron!' (There is a record that in the early 1870s the sticks were thrown at a clay pipe in the mouth of a wooden effigy of an old woman.) The game of skittles was also played in the gardens of some public houses and darts and dominoes were popular in the bar.

The long walk home from The Tandem had then to be faced and by the time we turned into our street, patent shoes were covered with a film of white dust and socks were at 'half-mast'. After supper we were more than ready for bed, leaving mother to start the interminable preparations for Monday morning.

CHAPTER EIGHT

# COME OUT TO PLAY

The first day of the working week was as unpopular then as it is now, but once school or work was finished, the rest of the day was ours. I had several friends from nearby houses and often in the evenings, though never on Sundays, we met in the street to play whatever game was then in season. In the spring it was whips and tops, three kinds: window-breakers, which could and often did; carrot tops, on which we drew designs with chalk; and drummer tops, a fatter version of the carrot. Later in the year we bowled hoops up and down the street, hoops of wood for girls and iron hoops and steers for boys, or festooned the roadway with skipping ropes. There were many rhymes connected with the latter: 'Salt, mustard, vinegar, pepper', followed by a quick turn of the rope. One was expected to jump touching the ground only once between every two twirls: these jumps were known as 'bucks'.

> Blackcurrant, redcurrant, raspberry tart,
> Tell me the name of your sweetheart.

Here, the rope was twirled quickly and one jumped to the chanting of the alphabet; the letter chanted when a foot tripped in the rope was taken as the first letter of a girl's or boy's name, supposedly one's sweetheart. This was quite a long game and progressed:

> Whom will you marry? – Rich man, poor man, beggar man, thief.
> When will you marry? – Sunday, Monday, Tuesday [and so on].
> What will you wear? – Silk, satin, muslin, rags.

There were several versions of this rhyme.

Jumping the rope was also popular, starting off at a reasonable height and rising to a high level which necessitated a rather unladylike method of 'monkey-jumping'. This was more or less a cartwheel and I, being caught in mid-air, as it were, by my scandalized mother, was taken indoors and

49

from then on 'monkey-jumping' was banned: 'Never mind what Janet Smith does, you are not to do it.'

Another difference of opinion took place between mother and me over the shoes I wore for skipping: 'How can I skip and do bucks in those old high boots, my shoes are much lighter', I complained.

But no, shoes were for Sunday wear, the button boots for everyday and mother won that battle, as indeed she had to, for children's footwear was expensive and to save money my father sat many evenings before a foot iron, repairing our boots, cutting and shaping the leather for sole and heel, polishing the edges with heel ball and finally, for good measure, hammering home a few 'Blakeys' at heel and toe.

During the course of a skipping game it was sometimes necessary to lower the rope to the ground to enable the odd horse and cart to pass or to avoid tripping the street singers. These were poor and homeless families who walked the streets singing for money. Sometimes the whole family would saunter down the middle of the road with mother and father trailing their weary children and taking turns to sing. Tramps, too, were a common sight in the streets, making their way from one casual ward to another. Often they would knock on our door quite early in the morning asking for a hunk of bread and a refill of tea in a billy-can. They were never sent away empty-handed; for many of these men were ex-service men who had been promised 'a land fit for heroes'. Sometimes they would stretch out on the rough grass of the Green to rest or to eat their meagre meal, but they were not moved on, rather were they a source of interest to the children whose playground it was, and their short respite was enlivened by cheery conversation and curious questioning. Of this fraternity I remember Percy, a young man whose speech indicated a good education, yet he was shabbily dressed, wore no shoes and spent his days 'on the road'. Another wanderer roaming the streets was Rhubarb, who, regrettably, because of his habit of rummaging in ash-boxes, was teased derisively and cat-called by children.

When the road was freshly tarred and gravelled, rope games were impossible. Heaps of gravel and sand lay at intervals down the street to be hand-shovelled on to the road on top of the wet tar, raising a cloud of dust. No matter how careful one might be, this tar adhered to shoes and clothing and was a great nuisance to housewives. Drains were opened by a hook and the evil-smelling silt collected with a long-handled scoop into a refuse cart, and during the long hot summer days the water-sprinkling cart, fitted with a galvanized container, would spray the road in an effort to lay the dust. Sometimes, in the case of severe illness, workmen would lay straw on the road near the house where sick people lay, to deaden sound from the street.

However, there was always 'Tig', or 'Hide and Seek'. If an 'It' or 'He' was required there was an assortment of rhymes chanted to a ring of children by one standing in the centre and pointing to the others in turn:

> One potato, two potatoes, three potatoes, four,
> Five potatoes, six potatoes, seven potatoes more.
> So out you go for saying so.

Alternatively:

> As I went down Icky-Picky lane,
> I saw three Icky-Picky children.
> What were they dressed in,
> Red, white or blue?

The child indicated would choose a colour – blue!

> B.l.u.e. spells blue,
> So out you go for saying so.

So, by process of elimination, children left the ring and the lone survivor was accorded the privilege of being 'It'.

A rhyme often thoughtlessly chanted was:

> Get a bit of pork,
> Stick it on a fork,
> And give it to a ju-ju baby,

arising from the annual holiday visit to Oxford of Jewish children from the east end of London. These children were housed among families who had volunteered to have them for one or two weeks and a midday meal of kosher food was provided and served to them at Cowley. Despite curiosity and a few preliminary scraps (though the London children were well able to look after themselves), friendly integration took place and the taunting was shortlived.

Another game was hopscotch, with several variations, the most common of which was a frame of squares in two rows of three chalked out on the roadway and numbered one to six. Starting at number one, the aim was to hop, at the same time kicking a smooth stone or tile into each square in turn, the second time round starting at number two and so on. If the tile finished on a line, the hopper was out and an opponent took over. We were fortunate that the roads were fairly quiet in those days and, even in summer, we were able to enjoy long spells at our games without interruption.

Terry Surman and friends examine the trenches on the rec.

Occasionally, we would cease play to watch and cheer on the chugging progress of a high two-seater car with canvas top; this car was familiar to us for it belonged to Dr Wylie.

In winter the old favourites of Ludo, Snakes and Ladders, Draughts and cards were much in use. My brother, a very methodical boy, whose books and toys were always in better condition than mine, was a collector of post-cards which he filed tidily away in albums; among these were some sent by my father during the 1914–18 war. These bore loving messages embroidered in coloured silks on organdie material which was secured to the card; they were very attractive and popular among the soldiers abroad. Sometimes Norman would shut himself in his room constructing cranes, lorries and other vehicles with his Meccano set, or spend hours with a John Bull printing set, laboriously setting the rubber type into a wooden frame. We were never left in doubt as to which were his possessions, for almost everything in his room was clearly rubber stamped with his name and address.

He had a large collection of cards then issued in sets of fifty with packets of cigarettes. The subjects were varied: kings and queens of England, fish, birds, ships, to name a few; and doubles were retained to swap with his friends or to play with. Probably one of the first sets of these cards depicted war generals and, oddly, from then on, whatever the subject, these cards were referred to as 'generals'. Sitting on the kerb in the street, each supplied with an equal number of cards, we would take it in turns to flick a card towards the front wall, attempting to cover completely the card of an earlier player. If successful, the two cards were claimed and in this way one player gradually acquired more cards than another and was declared the winner.

We also played 'hoop-la' with rubber rings from bottling jars, setting out on the pavement such trinkets or small articles as we could collect for prizes, and in the kerb itself we played marbles, trying to hit and so claim a marble previously played. These marbles were coloured and made of plaster, but the most prized possessions were 'Aggies' of clear glass enclosing a bright spiral of colour.

In the street or back garden fierce conker competitions took place and proud possessors of champion conkers would refer to their 'niner' or 'tenner' depending on the number of its conquests. Caps and guns were also popular, also the 'bomber', a round piece of lead about half an inch in diameter divided into two sections between which was placed a small pink cap. The lead was then swung on a string and dropped onto a hard surface which startled many an unsuspecting soul.

But these were chiefly boys' interests; I enjoyed painting and drawing and was reasonably useful with my needle and this led to my favourite occupation – dressing up. On the top of my wardrobe lay a large cardboard dress-box full of 'dressing-up things'; discarded lace curtains, ideal for fairy outfits, pieces of brightly coloured material, scarves, ribbons and a treasured tambourine. With any old clothes I could collect, plus a lot of imagination, it was possible to become a fairy, a gypsy or a nursery rhyme character, with the upstairs landing as a stage. Many a wet afternoon would find me floating from the bedroom adjoining the landing clad in a motley collection of garments, to sing and dance to my heart's content. Before me the banisters, and beyond a wall papered with a design of roses which became the faces of my audience to whom I performed in ecstatic oblivion of my real surroundings.

One of my dearest wishes was to take dancing lessons but as this was not possible on financial grounds, I made several attempts to fashion a pair of ballet shoes or 'toe' shoes as they were then known. Using the wooden shapes from empty date boxes, I fitted them into the cut-off toes of a pair of old felt slippers and padded hard with paper, fixing the whole thing to my feet with criss-crossed tape. Needless to say they were not successful and, after tripping down the stairs one day in these contraptions, I decided to settle for dancing pumps. These were soft black leather shoes without heels, black elastic crossing in front of the ankle and were very popular with little girls for parties and dancing. Ballet skirts were easily made from net curtaining, a long length of which I gathered fully about my waist by threading a ribbon through the top hem. With pins and rubber bands I fixed pieces of net to my shoulders and wrists, thus acquiring a magnificent pair of wings! If a meal-time interrupted my performance, I would sail downstairs at my mother's call and eat my dinner in full tinselled regalia; afterwards I would help to wash up, then return to the landing and my public!

This landing was a favourite spot with us if the weather outside was unkind. One Saturday, Norman, left in charge while my parents were out, spent his time dragging my sister and me up and down its length seated in the upturned top of mother's sewing machine, much to the detriment of the oil-cloth and the exasperation of our parents who were hard put to cope with the normal living expenses without needless repairs and renewals.

Some Saturdays we went with friends to the picture palace in Cowley Road, opposite Jeune Street (previously a theatre called the Empire, it had been supervised by Mr Albany Ward). Armed with boiled sweets and fruit we queued at the doors long before opening time, quite unnecessarily for there was a large auditorium, but there was always great competition to sit in the front row, again unnecessarily, for the picture was seen much more comfortably from a few rows back. The din must have been indescribable: each hero was cheered and each villain booed enthusiastically by those attending to the film. Those who were not, fought among themselves in the gangways or spent their time aiming orange peel at their enemies. The action was accompanied by a pianist below stage who varied the music to suit the mood or tempo of the film, which of course was silent and the action explained by captions. The price of this hectic afternoon out was a few pence only and deemed good value. The basement beneath the picture palace was used as a dance hall and was a hive of activity on Saturday nights.

When the Welshmen came to Oxford they brought with them their own sport and music, not only retaining it over the years but expanding it over the Oxford scene. A company of Oxford Welsh Glee singers was formed and they gave performances throughout the city and were enthusiastically received. There was already existing in Oxford at that time an organization known as the 'Health and Strength Club' for the promotion of physical training which attracted the membership of many Welshmen, and their impact on the club is probably best remembered by its instructor and founder, Mr Vic Couling, who has supplied the following information.

The Health and Strength Club was founded on 15 February 1925 and was associated with the Health and Strength League, a few local enthusiasts forming the initial membership. The headquarters was at the Grapes public house in George Street, Oxford, where a room over the bar was rented for two evenings per week.

Early in 1927, following the General Strike and its aftermath of labour disturbance, many Welsh people came to Oxford seeking employment at the Morris motor works. Many came from the Rhondda Valley, Blaengarw, Tonypandy, Pontypridd and Treorchy, place names which were to become familiar to Oxford folk in the years which followed.

The first Welsh visitor to make himself known to the Health and Strength Club was Stan Davies, a weight-lifter of repute, who was soon joined by his friend Billy Cooper, together forming an acrobatic act known as Chic and Conrad. Because of the new activities of weight-lifting and acrobatics it became necessary to move from the Grapes to an enlarged hut on the Cowley Road at the residence of member George Brooks, who, with his friend Gilbert Aries introduced boxing into the club curriculum. Welsh enthusiasts of physical activity soon swelled the membership of the club: the Williams brothers, Syd and Gwyn, Evan Morris, Gwyn Morgan, being amongst the boxers; while the gymnastic section under Billy Cooper soon had accomplished troupes giving displays at fêtes and concerts all over the district. As the troupes became more experienced, a break-away of the more skilled, five in number under Evan Harris, a pupil of Billy Cooper, formed an act entitled 'The Alfresco Five', and with Mr Couling as manager, secured engagements at the London Palladium, the Holborn Empire and for two weeks at the New Theatre, Oxford, appearing with Stanley Holloway and Lucan and McShane.

With more interest being taken in the club, which by this time had changed its name to the Oxford Physical Culture Club, new headquarters had been obtained at the Labour Hall, Pembroke Street. The weight-lifters

Cowley Road, Oxford, in the early years of the century

continued at Cowley Road and this side of the club work prospered under Stan Davies, with Ken Brookings joining him in holding records and several other local lifters gaining prominence.

The work of the club progressed and physical culture exhibitions were held at the Corn Exchange, Oxford, and in cinemas at Thame and Chipping Norton; while boxing matches were staged at the Iffley Institute (which became a temporary headquarters at one period). Larger varied entertainments were given at the Cowley Road Congregational Hall and one of the last big shows was held at the Carfax Assembly Rooms.

The associations of those past years were treasured by Mr Couling, for, as he observed: 'they brought a completely new aspect to many things in Oxford life'.

For our indoor amusement father constructed a 'cat's whisker' crystal set with the aid of a blueprint and what appeared to be yards and yards of wire – yet, to my astonishment, this was called a wireless set! There were two pairs of headphones and if the programme was of interest to us all, the ear-pieces were separated so that four people had one each. Favourite pro-grammes then broadcast from Station 2LO were Savoy Orpheans, Palm Court Orchestra, and Albert Sandler, the violinist. Later we acquired a radio powered by battery which meant almost weekly trips to a nearby shop to

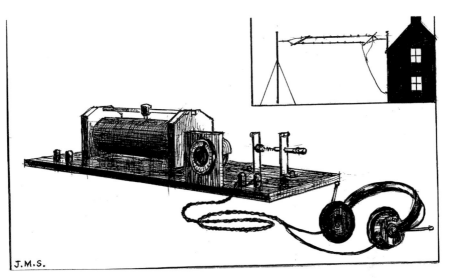

The homemade wireless set, 1922

get the accumulator recharged. These types of wireless involved having an aerial, a wire suspended the length of one's garden from two poles, as high as possible, but as these wires resulted in the untimely death of many homing pigeons, a popular hobby with some men, corks were threaded on to the wire at intervals to make it more easily visible to the birds. These wireless sets also had to be earthed by connecting them to a copper rod inserted in the ground.

With father thus employed at one end of the table, mother was seated at the other, sewing, ironing or rug-making, while we children were spread about on the floor engaged in our own devices. It was inevitable that we all occupied ourselves in the living-room during the winter months, for it was the only heated room. But seldom did our interests conflict, indeed, we often sang together as we worked. Mother would sing:

> Skylark, skylark, when you go up in the sky,
> If among the angels, mother you should see.
> Just ask her if she will come down again,
> To poor, dear daddy and me,

which unfailingly reduced me to tears, but father would cheer me up with, I think, the only song he knew completely – Nellie Dean – and we all joined in with gusto. Father's voice was strong and jolly, though hardly tuneful, so it was only to be expected that, on hearing he had volunteered to sing this song at a Christmas social, he should be told quite firmly by mother that singing at home was one thing, but in public, another – thus were father's theatrical aspirations curbed!

My mother also read to us frequently until we were able to do so for ourselves; my favourite spot for this during the long dark evenings was curled up in the big basket chair which stood by the fireside. The arms of that cushioned, creaking structure also comforted me through many a crisis of toothache, earache, or fit of temper. When eventually replaced by a modern, wooden armchair, it was given a glorious send-off on top of a bonfire on Guy Fawkes day.

In this way was spent such leisure time as the family had and the hours were few. Father worked from 7 a.m. to 6.30 p.m. for five days a week finishing at 2 p.m. on Saturday for an average weekly wage of £2, and at weekends he tended his allotment or did sundry repairs for neighbours to help the family exchequer. He travelled from job to job on an old bicycle which faithfully carried him and his tool-bag for many years, lighting his way in the winter with a small paraffin lamp, the glass front door of which opened to give access to the wick. As for mother, she had no set hours and in between coping with her housework and us children, she took in dressmaking to earn a little extra. She was also responsible for decorating the house when necessary, being much more nimble-fingered than her husband. She could paint and apply wallpaper almost like a professional and this was a much messier task then than nowadays. Paper was obtainable at about 8d. a roll and the adhesive, a paste made from flour and water, certainly effective but difficult to apply as any stray blobs appearing on the front surface of the paper left a permanent stain, so great care was necessary. Ceilings were usually brushed with a mixture of powdered whitening and water and dark-coloured paint was favoured because it did not show the dirt.

People were very concerned with durability and the economy of saving: old materials, towels etc., were saved and made up into face cloths, lavatory cloths and eventually dish and floor cloths, or simply used for polishing: they did not buy dusters. Waste not, want not, was their maxim.

# CHAPTER NINE

# SUPERSTITION AND BELIEFS

The interests and occupations so far described apply, in the main, to the ordinary people of Oxford; but Oxford has two faces, the City and the University, and the dividing line between Town and Gown was stronger in those early years of the 1920s than it is today. Members of the university mostly came from well-to-do families and were encouraged to remember this. Students were not allowed to frequent public houses in Oxford, though it must be admitted that some did. It was quite a common occurrence to see the robed University Proctor accompanied by his marshal enter such establishments while his 'bull-dogs' stationed themselves around the building to intercept any miscreant caught nipping over the back wall. Once inside, the Proctor would approach likely-looking groups of young men and enquire: 'Excuse me gentlemen, are there any members of the University here?' If the answer was negative he would apologize and withdraw, but if affirmative, he would ask for name and college and arrange an interview in his study the next morning. For this offence the defaulter would probably be fined.

The behaviour of undergraduates was often rowdy at the expense of Oxonians and their loud, exaggerated speech, often represented as the 'Oxford' accent, would have been better qualified as the 'Oxford University' accent, for it was not the true local dialect. Fortunately, with maturity, this exaggeration toned down, resulting in pleasant, clearly spoken English.

Local people tended to use the long 'a', to clip their words and to omit the double 't' in such words as better and butter. Neither were they too much concerned with grammar; I recall hearing the following reply to my father's polite enquiry:

59

'How are you George?'

'I be tolerable well, but me feet be allus bad!'

We had a neighbour from a nearby street, well known for her kindness in time of trouble despite her own obviously straitened circumstances: a large lady, ungainly in a shapeless mackintosh, she was rarely seen without a battered pram full of small grubby children, yet her stock reply to a greeting was a cheerful: 'Wotcher!' and I'm afraid that to us children she became 'Mrs Wotcher'.

Conversation was difficult with another of our acquaintances for he seldom finished a sentence, but tailed off with 'the whatsit' or 'the thingummy', leaving his listener to make what sense he might of the intelligence.

Much of this has been changed by modern methods of education, and at Sister Alice's school our elocution was swiftly taken in hand: faather became fahther, caastle became cahstle, and reownd the heowses became the more open rownd the howses. A triumph for the purists no doubt, but, as today's educationalists seem more inclined to preserve regional speech, let us hope that we in Oxford have not entirely lost ours.

But, accent or no, we were quite articulate, with a wide choice of sayings, superstitions and beliefs for which we had a healthy respect. Some beliefs stemmed from common sense, others, from fear or ignorance, merely survived from generation to generation by custom and word of mouth. Today there may be many who scoff and dismiss the subject of superstition as nonsense, but equally, are there not many who 'keep their fingers crossed', just in case?

We children attempted to attract good luck or repel bad luck in a variety of ways. To each other we would make such bragging statements as: 'I've not made one mistake in my sums', or: 'I've passed all my swimming tests first time', adding as an insurance against changing fortune: 'Touch wood'.

It was good luck to see someone wearing a straw boater, referred to by us as 'bashers'. Immediately one was sighted there was a cry of 'basher', accompanied by a lick of the right thumb, a quick touch of the left palm with the moistened digit, then the right fist was slammed into the left palm, and the first one to achieve this satisfying smack scored a point against her slower companion. Points were also awarded to the owner of the first pair of sharp eyes to spot a bearded gentleman in the street and cry 'beaver', or to the owner of the first finger to touch a sailor's collar. If, in error, we should don a garment inside out, this was lucky, and the garment so remained until the end of the day.

We went to great lengths to avoid incurring bad luck by walking under ladders, using the number thirteen, or opening umbrellas in the house. For the same reason we would never place boots upon the table, cut string from a parcel, or say 'thank you' to anyone picking up a dropped glove, and often chanted the following rhyme:

> See a pin and pick it up, all the day you'll have good luck,
> See a pin and let it lay, you'll have bad luck all the day.

We avoided looking at the new moon through glass, and instead went out into the garden to stand gazing at the shining crescent in the sky, at the same time turning a silver coin in an outstretched hand while making a wish. Silver coins were the half-a-crown, two-shilling piece or florin, a shilling commonly known as a bob, sixpence known as a tanner, and a small threepenny bit was a joey.

It was considered an ill omen if a bride setting out for the church encountered a funeral, but lucky indeed, and often so arranged by her relatives if, when leaving the church after the wedding, she should be greeted by a chimney sweep. After the reception she would drive off with her new husband in a vehicle behind which trailed on strings old boots and shoes tied there by well-wishers; while among the departing guests the young girls would take home a carefully wrapped portion of wedding-cake to be placed beneath the pillow at night: this was said to evoke dreams of a future lover.

Underneath a pillow was also the hiding place for the baby teeth of young children, in exchange for which it was hoped that the fairies would provide a silver sixpence.

Silver charms such as thimbles, small flat irons and threepenny bits were to be found by the lucky ones in the Christmas pudding and in our family two small china dolls, each about one inch long, were traditionally hidden in the pudding since my grandmother's day. When taking a bite of the first mince pie of the season, we would make a wish, and one old lady I knew always saved the holly from one year's decorations to burn on the fire beneath the big iron pan in which she boiled her puddings for the following year. If among any of our presents we were given anything with a cutting edge, such as scissors or a knife, we would immediately give to the donor a halfpenny, in the belief that this prevented the severance of a friendship. This relates to a book I once read which began: 'Uncross those knives Jemima!' the inference being that crossed knives meant an argument and, strangely, I can now never resist straightening crossed knives. Also at the table, a cup of tea with a large tea stalk floating on top was supposed to forecast a visit from a stranger, as was the presence of a bumble-bee in the house. And once the pot of tea was made, only the hostess was expected to pour; if any other female attempted this she would be stopped by warnings of 'ginger twins'. Spilled salt would be tossed over the left shoulder to guard against bad luck and hostesses would avoid if possible seating thirteen guests at a table.

Some superstitions arose from genuine situations. It was said that an old soldier would never light three cigarettes from one match, it having been estimated in the muddy trenches of France that this was just long enough for the light of the flame to betray the smoker's position to the Germans, thus making him an easy target for gunfire.

There was also good reason for upholding the ceremony of chimney-topping carried out by builders. It was expected that when a chimney stack was completed the builders should be supplied with beer as a prevention against a smoking chimney. It naturally followed that any parsimonious householder choosing to ignore this custom ran the risk of finding himself with a chimney which did smoke!

There were many beliefs connected with nature: black cats were lucky, as was a four-leaved clover, but we would never take flowering blackthorn or lilies into the house, and I was once told by a nurse that displays of red and white flowers in hospital were strongly discouraged. During a fishing expedition, the jam jar was never filled with water until the first fish had been caught: to do so would have meant, to our illogical thinking, no catch.

But many beliefs involving plants had a reasonable foundation based on their herbal properties: dock leaves were used to ease the rash caused by a stinging-nettle, water from boiled nettles or cabbage drunk to purify the blood, and goose-grease rubbed onto the chest to relieve congestion. Many were the remedies recommended to charm away warts, usually involving the burial of some object, such as an ear of corn or a piece of meat, with the promise that, as it rotted, so did the wart.

Then, as now, perceiving a glorious sunset, people would mutter:

> Red night, shepherd's delight,
> Red morning, shepherd's warning,

and hedges bedecked with an abundance of berries, hips and haws were assumed to be nature's provision for the birds in anticipation of a hard winter.

To emphasize a point, or a promise, we would say fervently: 'God's honour', or, holding up a licked forefinger:

> See it wet, see it dry,
> Slit my throat if I tell a lie.

In addition to these pledges and beliefs certain expressions were in use. Swearing was rarely heard among the children I knew, though adults had their own vocabulary for use when things went wrong: 'Drat' was commonly used as an expression of exasperation. Our greengrocer almost always referred to his horse as 'that dratted creature', though a more docile and inoffensive animal it would have been difficult to find. 'Oh blow' and 'Oh flick' were also used to let off steam, and the worst most parents said of tiresome children was that they were 'little hummers', 'little monkeys' or 'just plain ockard'.

Discipline was maintained in our house by dismissal upstairs or a sharp word: generally we recognized that if mother or father said 'no' that was it, sulk though we might; but I recall going to a party at one child's house and being fascinated by the sight of a cane hanging on a hook behind the door!

Sometimes a mother would say: 'Oh, you mammer me with your questions!' and my father would quell a persistently irritating child with 'Stop brevitting do!' which, though it had the desired effect, I thought a very puzzling word.

Another expression peculiar to my father was: 'You mustn't be a hothouse plant' and this was to encourage us out of the house into the open air he loved. I remember particularly one early morning in late summer, while mother was preparing breakfast, walking down the garden path, father's big hand holding mine, on the way to collect vegetables from the allotment. Around us the morning mist hung heavily after an overnight shower; cobwebs strung with pearls of dew spanned the path and broke at our passing; the air was full of the smell of ripening apples and antiseptic chrysanthemums as we passed through the little gate set in a dripping hawthorn hedge and on to the allotments. Before us the whole expanse was overhung with a damp haze in which, here and there, moved shadowy figures bent on a similar errand; behind us the street stirred, curtains were drawn back, wisps of smoke appeared from sleepy chimneys and the cock crowed in the garden run. The suction of rubber boots on mud made a satisfactory sound as we worked silently along the rows of vegetables, boots which afterwards had to be cleaned down with a rhubarb leaf and restored to a shiny blackness in the long wet grass which bordered the paths. Behind the houses the yellow light of the sun struggled with the mist, promising a fine day, and the green hedges drank greedily of the dew as sustenance against the coming heat. As I sat in the big wooden wheelbarrow among the muddy beetroot and the freshly pulled carrots waiting to be trundled home, father said to me: 'This, my love, is the pride of the morning.' And this time I knew what he meant.

63

# CHAPTER TEN

# FINE FEATHERS

Customs and beliefs were not the only things passed down through the family. From babyhood we were well clad in clothes of durable material which had survived much washing and had been handed down from one child to the next. Knitted matinée jackets and long white cotton or silk gowns, tucked and lace-trimmed, covered long, flannel petticoats, woollen vests and towelling napkins, and extra protection against the winter cold was provided by woollen shawls, woollen gaiters or leggings and knitted bonnets. This clothing applied to both sexes and, in fact, boys wore lace-trimmed, knee-length dresses until they were well over twelve months old, after which they were breeched into sailor suits, white or navy, with which they sported round sailor hats or large-brimmed straw hats.

With growing children the accent was still on durability, a boy's underwear was white vest and trunks under a thick flannel suit complete with waistcoat, usually grey for Sundays but always dark in colour. Sweaters were not common but some boys wore grey woollen long-sleeved jerseys with a high neck, buttoned on one shoulder. Shirts were usually plain, white or cream, and enhanced by a knitted striped tie. For school wear 'Sartor' raincoats were popular, usually navy in colour, with peaked caps, long woollen socks turned over at the knee and black laced boots.

Clothing for girls was more complicated. In the winter we were padded out with woollen vests, combinations and liberty bodices: white sleeveless jackets stitched with braid, buttoning down the front and from which, as we grew older, dangled four long suspenders for the support of long woollen stockings, black for weekdays, fawn on Sundays (smaller girls kept their stockings up with plain elastic garters). Winter knickers were fleecy, navy and clumsy, later to be replaced by knitted interlock in white, pale blue or pink. Dressing on cold winter mornings in an icy bedroom was an uncomfortable procedure, but Joyce and I devised our own method of overcoming this. Each night we placed our garments under the eiderdown to be ready for the small hands which, in the morning, emerged, grabbed and pulled them down into the warmth of the bed. Then we would sit up under the bedclothes, using our hands as tent poles and struggle into our underwear! The business of washing just had to be endured, then it was a quick dash to the fire downstairs, snatching up strategically placed top clothing as we fled.

Our winter coats were usually of tweed with fur collars and we wore 'Red Riding Hood' capes of rubber as protection against the rain. But in summer we wore lace-trimmed petticoats and knickers under short-sleeved cotton dresses; however, short sleeves were only for weekday wear; on Sundays to accompany straw hats and gloves, dresses were long sleeved and of silk, crêpe de Chine or voile, and worn with white knee-length socks and black patent shoes. We were more fortunate than boys in that our clothing was more colourful and cooler in summer for, although shirts were short sleeved and open necked, boys' trousers were still of thick white or grey flannel.

School wear for older girls was a pleated, navy serge gymslip with white long-sleeved blouse, black stockings, 'Sartor' raincoat and often a beret. These berets were very popular and available in many colours, with the additional advantage of being cheap, costing about 1s. 11¾d. In many haberdashery shops goods were priced to the third farthing; we would be asked for 'one and eleven three' or 'two and eleven three'. This practice sometimes led to difficulty when providing change and to overcome this shops would issue sheets of pins in lieu of a farthing. The guinea was a favoured price for the more expensive goods or for professional services.

Ladies rarely left the house for a journey without wearing a hat: large-brimmed felts, secured by long hat-pins, or later, tight-fitting 'cloche' hats which slipped snugly down into the fur collar of a winter coat. With their hats some older ladies wore black veils drawn down to cover the face

Ladies' and girls' fashions in 1926

completely, and in a later style short eye-length veils were suspended from the brim of the hat. Their dresses were in muted colours, long sleeved, low waisted, usually with a modesty vest – a detachable, rectangular piece of embroidered or lace material fitted into a V-neck.

A fashion advertisement of 1926 predicted that 'skirts will still be full, but this should be secured by circular cutting and hidden flares'. Wrap skirts were still favoured, also high Eton collars, fringes, floppy bows and cuffs, but 'the godet flounce will no longer be seen'.

Deep fuchsia was a colour much in vogue, with accessories of champagne hue and dresses for younger women became sleeveless with higher necklines and shorter skirts. The latter caused comment among the older generation, of course, but opinion upon the subject varied with age. A small boy asked what his new teacher was like replied: 'Powdered nose, semi-shingle, permanent wave, short skirt – oh, she's just topping!'

Of course, there were disadvantages: a man walking in Cornmarket saw a little girl crying and enquiring the reason for her tears was told:

'Mamma has gone across the road and left me.'

'Why didn't you catch hold of her skirt?' he said.

'Because I couldn't reach it,' was the reply!

Hemlines for older ladies were below the knee and legs, encased in grey or fawn lisle stockings, terminated in brown, grey or black shoes; but young ladies favoured 'silk chiffon hose with embroidered clocks at side at 6s. 11d a pair'.

Suits with long fitted jackets to the thigh and crocheted silk jumpers of similar length were very much in fashion and worn with long bead necklaces. Flower posies on the shoulder for evening wear and rings were much in favour; it was possible to buy diamond rings in gold settings for between 32s. and 3gns, and solid gold watch bracelets for 32s. 6d. Cheap watches were available from a local store for as little as 5s. and were perfectly satisfactory for a few years. From a similar store one might equip oneself with spectacles merely by trying on before a mirror and reading some sample typescript before deciding on a suitable pair costing 6d. per lens, plus 6d. for the frames. I once heard tell of an old gentleman who, too busy to go himself, sent his wife into this shop to choose a pair of spectacles for him!

Fur was very fashionable and used to trim collars and cuffs, though a preference for feather trimming shortly followed. The more affluent wore a full-sized animal skin which, with dangling legs, was draped around the shoulders and secured in front by a clip so that the animal's mouth appeared to open to grasp the tail. My mother did not possess such an article of finery, but she did have a smaller version which she called a tippet. Almost without exception, underneath all this top clothing women were encased in corsets, pink or white creations, stiffened with whalebone or metal strip and

'Suits with long fitted jackets...'

with laces back and front, so that the imprisoned body might be squeezed and eased into an acceptably fashionable shape. In Victorian times young girls were automatically introduced to this garment whether its supposed figure-correcting properties were needed or not and it is not surprising, therefore, that as women grew older, their muscles became reliant upon its support so that they felt uncomfortable without it. A newspaper advertisement of 1926 reads:

F. Cape & Co.
Our special reducing model with patented cross supports in strong contil. Fitted with rustless and unbreakable 'Twilfit' spiral steels and six patented rubber grip hose supports. In dove or white 15/11d.

Newspaper was used by ladies to test the heat of their curling tongs, resulting in a pile of discarded newsprint, corrugated by scorch marks. Special salons for ladies' hairdressing were now beginning to appear and shorter styles such as the 'bob', 'shingle' or 'Eton crop' replaced the 'bun' or 'earphones'. Inevitably these cropped styles were regarded by some with disfavour:

> The shingle, like many a fashion before it, has been adopted by those it suits and those who should pass it by – they are those with thick necks which shorn locks cannot hide; heads which are flat at the back; and very thin faces which would be better set off by coils of hair over the ears!

Cosmetics were little used except by the wealthy, though perhaps a little dab of eau-de-cologne behind the ear was permitted!

Men's suits were also dark in colour: jacket, waistcoat and trousers which came up above the waistline at the back into two points. At the end of each point was a button to which one end of a pair of braces was secured and the other carried over the shoulders to button on the front of the trousers. Flannel trousers were available at 21s. a pair, socks at 2s. 6d. a pair, and pyjamas at 6s. 6d. Sometimes instead of, or even with, a waistcoat, men wore pullovers, priced at around 8s. 6d to 13s. each. Working shirts were of striped flannel and best shirts of white cotton with detachable collars, back and front collar studs and cufflinks; but occasionally the collar was dispensed with and replaced by a silk scarf twisted twice round the neck and knotted in front. This clothing hid long woollen underpants and sleeved vests which fastened in front with linen buttons. Socks were woollen and calf length as they were generally worn with boots. Caps were favoured for work but, on Sundays, trilby hats together with raglan style raincoats were the thing to wear. With the advent of the Welsh miners came a new fashion. Caps and mufflers for work of course, but on Sundays, a smart suit, the most notable feature of which was the double-breasted waistcoat cut straight across the lower front. This style was copied and much favoured by the young men but was not approved by their more provincial parents.

Dress for men changed little with age, but grandmothers had a style all their own. Almost always in black, they wore attractive bonnets, creations of silk, feathers and jet beads, tied under the chin, together with short capes similarly decorated. Skirts were ankle length, from the hem of which peeped out black, shiny toe-capped shoes or boots. Their dresses had tight bodices, tucked and embroidered, with narrow lace trimming at the throat; sleeves were always long and fastened into a cuff, for these ladies were the product of a narrow-minded age when it was considered daring to display an ankle, and bare arms were reserved for the wash-tub.

Although this restricted outlook was beginning to ease, we children always wore hat and gloves when leaving the house for any length of time, particularly on Sundays. Indeed, every member of the family distinguished between working and Sunday clothes. In every wardrobe 'best' clothes hung on a hanger during the week and were taken out only on Sundays or for special events such as weddings or funerals. New clothes started off as 'Sunday best', being relegated to working clothes as their condition deteriorated; but wool, serge and flannel were materials with long life expectancy and stood up to a great deal of patching and darning so that new clothes were something of an event. Ready-made children's clothing was, apart from underwear, not in great demand; most mothers made clothes for their youngsters either from new material or by cutting, turning and refashioning old garments. For those unskilled in this art help was at hand, as seen from the following advertisement, dated August 1920:

A course of lessons in Practical Dressmaking. The object being to teach every lady and young girl to make their own dress, blouse etc., and to cut out economically and correctly. Fee 2/6d per lesson.

Sewing was a main subject at Sister Alice's school, and I spent many hot afternoons painstakingly forming french seams, and run-and-fell seams, on stiff calico material, my laborious progress marked by little spots of blood where the needle dug deeply!

# CHAPTER ELEVEN

# SHOPS AND TRADERS

My attendance at Sister Alice's necessitated a walk through neighbouring streets, so that I became completely familiar with the area and was quite reliable in the matter of shopping for mother which I did on Saturday mornings. This locality abounded with small general stores which appeared to stock every commodity; such a shop was James's. This little shop stood on a corner in Charles Street, its exterior walls plastered with enamelled advertisement plates extolling the virtues of such things as Bryant and May matches and Brooke Bond tea, and its front path was bounded by a high brick wall on one side and on the other, behind the front railings, a gravelled space giving access to the shop window. Few people could enter the shop at a time for every available space on its walls, door and counter was occupied by samples of the multitude of goods offered for sale. On a scrubbed wooden counter, loaded with bottles and boxes, stood a set of brass scales, for most goods, sugar, fats and so on, were weighed loose and then wrapped. Flour was sold in cotton bags and these were saved, boiled and used for many purposes such as straining fruit when making jelly. Sweets lay uncovered in the window regardless of hot sun or flies: sweethearts, tiger-nuts, licorice, jelly-babies and Sharp's creamy toffee, while on the floor, at the base of the counter, stood large sacks opened to display corn meal, maize and dog biscuits, flanked by a barrel of vinegar or a can of paraffin. Stamps, soap, notepaper, cheese, fruit, kindling wood and Union Jack corn plasters, all could be procured from James's.

Next door, fronting Catherine Street and also owned by the shopkeeper, was a bakery from which wafted daily the delicious smell of freshly baked bread. Sometimes I would be sent round with a newly mixed dough cake for baking, its surface crowned with a small piece of grease-proof paper on which was written our surname. This was a service provided by the baker for a few pence; he would also cook Sunday dinners for local people, and a similar service was provided by Hudson's bakery in Hertford Street.

Mrs Lisemore lived next door to the bakery. She made, and sold from her front room, toffee apples, sweets of many varieties, big trays of cold rice

RICE PUDDING

BREAD PUDDING

Mrs Lisemore's rice and bread
pudding

pudding which she cut into slices, and wads of bread pudding. I remember
her as a very clean and homely lady, quite skilled in the culinary arts.

Also in Catherine Street was Batten's shop which one entered up two steps,
announced by the clang of a spring bell. This shop was a delight at Christmas:
coloured lights reflected on the tinselled decorations and a large selection of
small toys and gifts attracted noses to the window glass and extracted pennies
from their safe-keeping in a woollen glove. Mr and Mrs Batten also introduced us to the delights of Vantas, an aerated liquid mixture of orange and
lemon which was drunk on the premises. In common with many local shops
Batten's also ran a Christmas club. Commencing early in the year one paid
over a few pence or whatever could be spared each week: this amount was
entered on a card by the shopkeeper and the resulting sum could be spent on
goods from his shop. This was a popular way of saving with many families.

The nearby Magdalen Road boasted quite a shopping centre. Here, from
a little newspaper shop rendered almost impenetrable by its well stocked

counter and hanging display-racks of papers and periodicals, I obtained my weekly comic, and the smell of that freshly printed paper remains in my memory still; true, the colouring and the drawn figures were not always in unison, but, no matter, the magic was there. *Rainbow, Bubbles,* and *Tiger Tim,* each costing 2d., weekly recorded the exploits of Jumbo, Jacko, Bobby Bruin, Georgie Giraffe, Joey the Parrot, Fido and other animal characters presided over by a permanently harassed Mrs Bruin, whose hands seemed for ever raised heavenwards in exasperation at their antics.

There was a butcher, a fishmonger, a small haberdasher and a big junk store known as Cleaver's. If one needed a piece of wood, iron, odd model aeroplane wing or wheels for a trolley, this was the place to go. The whole yard was a glorious jumble of rubbish and junk, yet Mr Cleaver knew exactly where to look for a required article. Adjoining the yard was a small dark shop where Mrs Cleaver sat all day behind a counter covered with the more delicate goods: necklaces, bracelets and stuffed birds.

In complete contrast was the establishment of their near neighbour, Smart Faulkner's grocery shop. Entering by double doors the customer walked onto a floor daily strewn with fresh sawdust and the assistants wore spotless white coats and white, deep-fringed aprons, reaching almost to the floor. Here one was offered a high, cane-seated chair and given individual attention.

Assistants in long aprons,
White, fringed along the hem.
Greeted me with a smile,
And so I smiled at them.
One offered me a little chair,
Cane-seated, long of leg.
Which I accepted gratefully,
And then of him did beg,
Half-a-pound of best butter,
He took his wooden pats,
Selected just the right amount
From one block of the fats.
This he shaped with nimble flicks
And cheerful patting sound.
On greaseproof sheet the butter lay,
With thistle pattern crowned.

Goods were paid for over the counter, the money with the bill was put into a small container which was then slotted into an overhead wire and, by the

'... such a shop was James's'

pull of a handle, sent spinning along the wire to a central, raised cash desk, where it was emptied, refilled with change and receipt and returned to the assistant by the same method. This cash railway held great fascination for me and I used to envy the cashier perched high in her eyrie and admire the efficient way in which she effected the exchange and the assurance with which she sent that little container twanging on its way. Shop assistants worked long hours in those days, often till 8 p.m. or 9 p.m., the busiest night being Saturday after the weekly pay-day. During the 1914–18 war, queues would form outside this shop, or Warner's in Hertford Street, when it was known that black treacle was on sale.

In Magdalen Road also was situated Witham's shop, selling such delicacies as faggots and peas, pigs' trotters, chitterlings and tripe, and next door the Mission Hall, which during the 1914–18 war had opened as a soup kitchen from whence a jug of steaming hot soup could be purchased for one halfpenny. The gentleman in charge of the hall was Mr Henry Clifford, the City Missionary and a much respected member of the community – so much so that, in February 1920, referring to the raising of a testimonial to him by the City in commemoration of his thirty years of social work, the vicar of SS Mary and John, writing in the parish magazine, was moved to comment:

Mr Clifford is not a churchman, and we certainly don't want our people to run off to his Mission Hall. On the other hand, Mr Clifford is a man whom we all respect, and who has done a great deal of social work among us. He has been an active and useful member of our Relief Committee and he has worked hard and well for the Charity Organisation Society and is a Poor Law Guardian.

This was a tribute indeed and well deserved.

Sometimes a small newsagent or haberdasher would reserve a corner of his shop as a sub-post office: one such stood on the corner of Leopold Street and Hurst Street and was known as Clarke's. Postage then cost a $1\frac{1}{2}$d. for a postcard and 2d. for a letter and there were several deliveries and collections each day. But our nearest post office was on the Iffley Road just round the corner from Howard Street. In the garden of a large house owned by the Shirley family, an extension had been erected under the trees and here Mr Shirley would serve us with stamps, postal orders and so on, and deal with all matters relevant to our mail.

The *Oxford Mail* evening newspaper was delivered to our house by 'Old Mo', a short, elderly man who appeared to be in poor circumstances for he was shabbily dressed in long raincoat and battered cap. Possessor of an alarming, bronchial cough, which could in no way have been helped by the weary cigarette which hung from his lower lip, he could be heard many yards away wheezing his way through the darkness, rain and winter fogs to deliver his papers. Such was the need in those days: work or go without.

Newspapers were never thrown away but taken periodically to the nearby fish and chip shop where they were used to wrap the purchases of a 'tuppenny' and a 'pennorth'. Our fish and chip shop, further down the street, was a flourishing concern even in summer, but in winter, despite fog and rain, a queue often formed outside the shop. Once inside, the aroma of the sizzling oil made the wait worthwhile. It was a pleasure to watch the pale, white potatoes placed one at a time under the chipper and to see the uniform sticks tossed into the deep sea of brown, boiling oil, to emerge some minutes later, crisp, golden brown, and piled alongside a succulent piece of fried fish; or to shake the vinegar bottle vigorously over a greasy bag of scrumps: small particles of crisply fried batter. I rarely saw the face of the lady of the establishment, her eyes seemed permanently fixed on the bubbling expanse before her and it was her husband who took the orders and handed over the moist warm bundles of newspaper. Consequently, whenever the door bell clanged she would call out: 'Goodnight, thank you', regardless of whether a customer had entered or left!

Many goods or services were advertised in the local newspapers or magazines, and very politely too. Messrs F. Cape & Co., a large drapery firm

Cowley Road in about 1910

promised 'delivery of the goods in a few minutes' and Webber's of Oxford offered 'necessary alterations, free of charge' and 'carriage paid on all parcels'. The City Juvenile Employment Committee advertised 'thirteen weeks training course for unemployed girls 16–18, thirty hours per week, free training and maintenance of ten shillings per week [instead of unemployment pay]', but for the more frivolous, private lessons in ballroom dancing, including the five step and tango, were offered.

A little further afield from Magdalen Road lay the Cowley Road shops; one of these near the Plain was occupied by a watch repairer by the name of Ganter. His establishment had no shop window, but was merely set up in the front room of his house. The walls of this dark little room were hung with clocks and watches of all kinds, and behind an old wooden counter, almost buried by varied specimens of horology, was a head: I never saw Mr Ganter stand up in all my visits there. He was a childhood acquaintance of my father who often recounted with glee the tale of an occasion when he took a watch in for repair and the following conversation took place:

'I've brought back this watch which you sold me, it cost half-a-crown, now it's stopped!'

Mr Ganter, after examining the watch said:

'How long have you had this then Harry?'

'Twenty-five years.'

'Then I'll repair it for nothing for your cheek!' exploded Mr Ganter.

In addition to the shops, a great deal of trade was carried on in the streets by hawkers, or door-to-door salesmen. Bread came round in horse-drawn vans, not wrapped or sliced, but crusty and golden brown, fresh from the oven, for there were no big multiple bakers and all baking was done locally by small firms. A certain baker who delivered around the streets near my home drove a small two-wheeled horse-drawn cart and, having a reputation for 'liking his drop', he earned for himself the nickname of 'Tiddley'. Some wit remarked that he delivered only to pubs and, be that as it may, it was certainly widely appreciated that at the end of the day it was the horse who took him home!

Fresh fish and rabbits were also brought round the streets by horse and cart transport. Most of these sales were cash transactions but this particular vendor had a novel and effective way of extracting his money from slow-paying customers: when polite request failed, he would poke a fish's head through the letter box of the offender's front door!

Local farmers delivered milk in large tinned-steel churns to various small dairies throughout Oxford; our nearest was the Oxford Dairy in Little Percy Street, and from here the delivery men would set out, each with a small truck carrying one or two churns, crying as they went 'Milk-O'. This was the signal for householders to come out with their jugs which were then filled from half- or one-pint measures. These measures, hanging around the cart on hooks, were also made of tinned steel and banded with brass, as were the churns, and the whole apparatus gleamed and shone with cleanliness. Was it my imagination, or were milkmen always cheerful men with rosy cheeks ready for good-humoured backchat with their customers, enduring the hot summer sun without complaint and the bitter winter winds with hands blue and stiff with cold? I recall two such stoical milkmen, Mr Belcher from Dorchester, and Mr Mattingly who ladled out skimmed milk from churns which he transported by horse and cart. Horses were generally well cared for by tradesmen and well trained, moving gently from door to door without instruction, knowing by experience where stops were to be made. I once saw a little girl run out into the road and fall before Mr Mattingly's horse: the animal reared immediately on to its hind legs, turning away from the child before the forelegs were lowered to the ground, so no harm was done. Local milkmen were also very generous, donating free supplies of milk to church whist drives and Christmas and Poor Law parties.

Another familiar figure delivering to our house in all weathers, his head protected by a hood fashioned from a split sack, was the coalman who also owned a small, grubby general store, adjoining which was a stable and, by contrast with his store, the animals – big shire horses – were beautifully cared for. When the coalman stopped work to eat his midday sandwiches,

Bricknell's shop in Catherine Street. In the window is a poster advertising films at the Palace cinema in Cowley Road

the horse was not forgotten, but provided with a nosebag full of hay, suspended from its neck at such a level that it could munch contentedly from the bag as and when it chose. It was said of this coalman that he once sold one of these animals and when it was later reported to him that the beast was being ill treated, he immediately called on the purchaser and insisted on buying back the horse! Until about 1912 he would enter his horses, groomed and decorated, in May Day processions with notable success and although these gatherings ceased shortly after this date he would still, on the first day of May, adorn his horses with coloured flowers and rosettes and entwine their plaited manes and tails with red, white and blue ribbons.

Coal was then the fuel most commonly used for heating a house – I was often set the task of counting the hundredweight bags as they were delivered – but, because of strife in the mining industry during this period, supplies were not always easily obtained as will be seen from the following advertisement:

Best coal – cash down. 60/2d a ton.

I should esteem it a favour if you would give me a week's notice as I find very great difficulty in getting supplies along.

In 1921, the same merchant was urging early orders 'because of a coal strike' and by 1925 his message to customers read: 'Prices withdrawn until further notice', and in 1926 he was merely accepting orders for delivery, 'when the coal strike is settled'.

Other carts toured the streets selling salt, large blocks of it, from which, on request, pieces were cut off and weighed before sale; and, according to season, one well-known old lady would walk the streets pushing before her a big handcart on the upturned handle of which she rested both arms as she called her wares. In winter it was 'Wood blocks' and in summer 'Ripe bananas'.

On Sunday mornings we were assailed by a cry of 'Watercress' from a man laden with baskets of watercress, but generally, supplies of fruit and vegetables came to us on a horse-drawn cart owned by a greengrocer from Littlemore. As business prospered, this gentleman decided to mechanize his transport and invested in a motor lorry. This was fine for the journey from Littlemore to our locality but, once arrived, he appeared to find the vehicle less accommodating than his old horse. Abandoning the effort of starting and stopping the engine every few yards, he would release the brake and with much straining and perspiration push it on to his next port of call. Perhaps the horse, gently grazing in a field at Littlemore, had the last laugh!

Periodically, a collector of glass jars and bottles appeared in our road pushing a truck, the sides of which were gaily adorned with paper windmills which he would exchange for a jam jar. Needless to say, he had no difficulty with his collection for what mother could resist the appeal: 'Got a jam jar mum?'

The cry of 'Knives to grind', brought out the folks with their blunt equipment, shears and scythes. The grinder, of swarthy complexion, had a big carborundum wheel fixed on the handlebars of his bicycle which he supported on a stand. Then, sitting on the saddle, he would start pedalling which caused the carborundum to rotate and the rasping metallic noise at the impact of revolving wheel with implement was accompanied by bright, gold sparks which flew out in all directions.

Very colourful characters seen then in the streets were the gypsies with their baskets of pegs and paper flowers: not the now favoured spring-clip pegs, but pegs made from two slivers of willow with two ends tightly bound together by a strip of metal, so that the opposite ends parted slightly to allow for the thickness of the material to be pegged. Brown-skinned, with wrinkled faces, the origin of their native country in doubt, these gypsies engendered a certain amount of fear so that children would run indoors at their coming despite low, wheedling reassurances that all would be well because: 'You've got a lucky face dearie'.

A display of bicycles and electrical goods at a 1930s trade fair in the Town Hall

Also of gypsy stock was 'Johnny Onion'. These men were often to be seen around Oxford streets and from the handlebars of their bicycles hung long strings of onions which they attempted to sell from door to door. In their berets and coloured neckerchiefs, they resembled the inhabitants of the Latin quarter of Paris, but in reality, their origins were much less romantic.

Incongruous, turbanned figures, supposedly from the mystic east, some-times came to the door, weighed down with huge cases of silks or satins, or carrying over the shoulder rugs and carpets of oriental design. So quiet and polite were they that I felt sorry for them and regretted that mother never bought their wares. Sometimes they brought pins and cottons, ribbons and general haberdashery and they were more successful with the sale of these, particularly in the case of one old lady, a neighbour, who bought often from one such Indian salesman and even if she needed nothing would pass the time of day with him. When she died, her family were touched to see him standing outside the house as her coffin left; he had come to pay his respects according to his way of life.

Another foreign-looking visitor was often to be found at the junction of Catherine Street and Percy Street, a moustachio'd Italian gentleman who regaled us with the sound of his barrel-organ.

But many of the street hawkers were local people: the ragman, shattering the peace of the neighbourhood by the violent ringing of his bell and his hoarse cry of 'Rag-an-bones'. With his horse and trolley this collector would buy old rags, bones, rabbit skins and the like for a few pence. Whether this was a profitable undertaking is difficult to say for he always appeared to have clothed himself from his stock!

Ice-cream was made locally, often in private houses, but was sold only in the summer months. A great favourite was Mr Bull who toured the area with his brightly painted two-wheeled box-cart which held two metal canisters of ice-cream and from each corner of the cart rose a twisted brass pole supporting a gaily striped canopy. Periodically he would rest his cart on its two wooden back legs and proceed to distribute his wares to his clamouring customers; though elderly and quiet, he was fortunately very tolerant of children. A cloth cap covered his greying hair, and a white moustache his smiling mouth, while his thin, wiry body was enveloped in a spotless white apron. At lunchtime he would stop in the centre of the crossroads by St Alban's church and take, from a little wooden box between the handles of his cart, a brown paper bag of sandwiches. This was his dinner and I was always amazed that he should prefer this when before him were two tubs of such delicacy. The ice-cream, it must be admitted, was more like frozen custard but, sold in one penny cornets or halfpenny boats it was in great demand. (Later this gentleman was replaced by the 'Stop-me-and-buy-one' vehicles. These were tricycles adapted to carry an ice box between the front wheels and were propelled by men in smart, blue-and-white striped jackets and peaked caps. This ice-cream was far superior in quality, sold wrapped in silver paper and produced under much more hygienic conditions.) Mr Bull was, more often than not, the recipient of my pocket money which was one penny a week and known as the 'Saturday penny', plus anything else I might acquire. However, I learned to be thrifty and often spent it in farthings, for five aniseed balls for a farthing, a pomegranate, or a long strip of licorice lasted so much longer than an ice-cream.

I have heard tell of other salesmen who pounded these streets during the first decade of the twentieth century. The bell of the Muffin-man often rang out a welcome call, and a little man in dark clothes with a tall hat which sprouted rolled fly-papers was commonly heard crying:

> Oh those tormenting, tickling flies,
> Catch 'em all alive, alive,
> Catch 'em alive,

but he had disappeared before the days of my memory.

# CHAPTER TWELVE

# St Alban the Martyr

We were not, however, concerned merely with the material things in life: from infancy we were taught to believe in God. Every night we would kneel by the bedside, hands clasped, eyes closed, to say our prayers. In the summer, probably the whole of the Lord's prayer would be recited, to which we would add requests for help with our own problems, but in the winter the bitter cold of our unheated bedroom usually reduced this procedure to a muttered: 'Thank God for a good day, Amen', before plunging into bed and the welcome warmth provided by a stone hot-water bottle. After a meal, it was hands together, eyes closed and a breathless: 'Thank God for a good dinner, Amen', before rushing off to some assignment; and if this little ceremony was overlooked we were called back to rectify matters. I was always rushing off somewhere and my father would sing:

> Fidgety Phyl,
> Can't sit still.

Every Sunday we went to the morning service and catechism in the afternoon at our local church of St Alban the Martyr which stood in Charles Street on a corner opposite James's shop. Built partly of brick, partly of sheets of corrugated iron painted green, it had a red-tiled roof and was approached by a steep concrete slope, at the top of which one turned left into the porch. Very dark and gloomy inside, it was, nevertheless, well attended. About halfway between the entrance door and the chancel on the south side stood the life-sized, or so it seemed to me, carved and decorated figure of St Alban. The sun's rays penetrating through the window behind him illuminated the splendour of his Roman centurion's uniform and I must admit to spending much of my time admiring him when I should have been attending to the sermon.

Another distraction was encouraged by the fact that boys and girls were not allowed to sit together in church: the girls sat on the north side and the boys on the south, but this did not prevent the exchange of grimaces, some smirking, others threatening, across the central aisle. The service was regarded as 'high' but the pageantry of the ceremony held our attention for some time, after which we would sit on the floor between the pews swapping treasured pieces of silver paper with our neighbour. It was our habit to collect silver paper from Easter eggs and other sources, smooth it out and keep it pressed in our prayer books. I am sure that the teacher knew of this activity but at least it kept us quiet, and something of the lesson must surely have rubbed off. Indeed, there was little disciplinary trouble during the service; Miss Daisy Randall, Mrs Smith, Mrs Eden and other teachers had us well in hand and, during Communion, the incense-laden atmosphere and the silence broken only by the occasional tinkling of a bell were impressive enough to awe us into rigidity.

On certain occasions our priest, Father Hayward, a fine-looking man, tall, well built and with grey hair, resplendent in lace-trimmed surplice and robes and preceded by a server swinging incense, would lead his singing

The choir of St Alban the Martyr

A wooden shrine with the
Howard Street roll of honour

choir, churchwardens and such members of the congregation as cared to
follow, around the local streets in procession, pausing in prayer before certain houses which displayed by the front door a wooden shrine. These
shrines made their appearance as a result of the 1914–18 war, sometimes
one to each street, recording the names of those of its residents on active
service. The small wooden gable and sheet of glass sheltered a Roll of
Honour on which was inscribed a list of names and regiments against some
of which were added, all too often, the initials R.I.P., and at the base of the
shrine stood a small pot of fresh flowers. (What appears to be the remains of
one of these shrines is still to be seen at the head of a grave in Littlemore
parish churchyard.)

During Holy Week there was outdoor preaching and we were told: 'We
shall want men to form a choir, a cornet, lanterns etc. We propose going
through half the parish each evening, the service to last one hour each time.'

Father Hayward was a much respected figure in the area. He visited many
houses to encourage, cheer or sympathize in times of stress or bereavement.

There were many sad cases of men still suffering from wounds, both in mind and body, sustained during the Great War of 1914–18. Cases of 'shell-shock' and 'gas' were common and regarded with puzzled curiosity by those of us too young to have experienced the horror of the trenches in France, but with maturity came the knowledge, the understanding and the pity. When a resident died the family drew all window blinds in the house until after the funeral and as the cortège left the house all neighbours would draw their blinds as a token of respect. Mourners wore black clothing, stockings, shoes and hats to the funeral and for some time afterwards, and wore on the left sleeve of coat or jacket a black diamond or black armband. The hearse, drawn by black horses, was a magnificent equipage with etched glass, silver fitments and a railed top to accommodate wreaths. Most burials took place at Rose Hill cemetery or in the churchyard of SS Mary and John.

Church activities were not confined to Sundays. At St Alban's we had our own house for the priest-in-charge and a church room in little Percy Street which was open most evenings for various functions, such as the Meccano club, the Thursday night social club, and for concerts and parties. Sunday school outings, for sometimes as many as one hundred persons, were orga-nized by the priest-in-charge and faithful supporters of the church such as Mrs Randall, Miss Daisy Randall, Miss Blackwell and Bert Neville, and a jolly time was had by all as evidenced below:

> We went off by motor lorry in two loads to the field kindly lent by Father Champion of Littlemore, where we had games and sports and then retired, with good appetites, to the Parish Room, also kindly lent, for tea.

And on another occasion:

> On August 21st 1920, the Lads' Guild, in a wagonette went to Dor-chester where, after a game of football on the recreation ground, we had tea at the George and then proceeded on to the Fair to try our luck at coconut shies and hoop-la etc.

It appears that the football club was a flourishing concern by 1924: 'St Alban's United Football Club is going along merrily. Out of nine league matches we have won five, lost three and drawn one. The ground is at Iffley. . .' and the guiding influence behind this team, known as 'The Vicar's Angels', was Sid Pipkin, himself a young man in poor health, obliged always to use crutches.

The church room was in constant use for winter sales, sales of work, and whist drives, for the parishioners were industrious and only by such means could they finance the needs of the parish, and the needs were many and varied. An appeal in November 1920 ran: 'We want a lamp to hang in front of the Altar, for use when the Blessed Sacrament is Reserved in the Tabernacle', and this must have met with immediate response, for in December: ' . . . the lamp is now in position. It is given by one of our communicants as a thank-offering.'

In January of the following year a rummage sale was organized:

> . . . with the proceeds we hope to get some new cassocks for the servers. Those we have at present have seen much service and somehow they don't grow with the lads, so we often have to squeeze quite a large-sized server into quite a small-sized cassock!

The lay needs of parishioners were not neglected. A bath chair owned by the parish was available for a rental of 2d. an hour, and there were advertisements for accommodation appearing in the parish magazine: 'Is there anyone who can let two rooms on the same floor to an elderly lady who is lame?' and a lost and found department: 'Found in the church room, a folding shoe-horn and button hook'.

Most of my early religious education took place at St Alban's, but as I grew older I often went with my family to evening service at St James's church, Cowley, and this was the church we almost always attended for the harvest festival, for then every sill, niche and corner was decorated with the fruit of many hours' labour in garden and allotment. The stone window sills, hung with ivy and red creeper, were filled with bowls of yellow and bronze chrysanthemums, their shaggy heads standing out like miniature mops against the soft varying purple of the Michaelmas daisy. Huge urns of gladioli and copper beech stood in the entrance to welcome the worshippers into the cool, shady church; foliage twined softly around the lectern or stood in stiff sprays around the pulpit. On the nave carpet, in front of the altar rails, lay the vegetables, large glossy green-striped marrows, pumpkins, potatoes carefully washed and arranged, big Bramley apples, strings of onions, and baskets or garden trugs full of beetroot and turnips. All this produce was later sent to homes and hospitals, but for one glorious Sunday evening it was displayed that we might all appreciate the blessings of a good harvest. This church, always well attended, excelled itself for this festival and the rafters rang with an enthusiastic rendering of 'We plough the fields and scatter, the good seed on the land'.

Probably one reason for the popularity of this church was the forthright manner of its vicar, the Revd George Moore, well known for his outspoken comments and unconventional behaviour – he had been known to interrupt a funeral service to chase his sexton out of the churchyard because a grave had been dug in the wrong place – and his clashes with officialdom were frequent and public; nevertheless, he held the living at Cowley from 1875 until 1928.

Sometimes we went to St Clement's church at the foot of Headington Hill, Oxford. My father had lived in St Clement's parish as a boy and had been a keen member of the Church Lads' Brigade and a regular worshipper at this church: consequently he had a thorough knowledge of, and respect for, the Bible, and could quote from it quite freely. It was at this church that I attended confirmation classes, though the actual ceremony took place in the city church of St Martin and All Saints, on the corner of Turl Street.

Religious instruction was also given at school. In the infants' it was mostly at morning assembly under the eagle eye of Miss Rogers. I can clearly recall standing on my allotted spot in the hall, eyes closed, palms together, fervently singing:

> Great Father of Glory, Pure Father of Light,
> Thy light in a mess Sybil, hid from our sight.
> All laud we would render, oh help us to see,
> 'Tis only the Splendour of Light hideth Thee

and it was not until we were given hymn books that I realized the error of my rendering of the second line of this hymn.

At Sister Alice's, scripture lessons started each day's curriculum and we attended church frequently, walking in crocodile from school to the church of St John the Evangelist on the Iffley Road; but in secondary school, although scripture was taught, there were no organized visits: it was, of course, expected that we attend our local churches on Sunday.

# CHAPTER THIRTEEN

# SS MARY AND JOHN

St Alban's was only one of a group of churches contained in the parish of Cowley St John. Of the others, the parish church of SS Mary and John standing on the corner of Leopold Street and Cowley Road, whose vicar, the Revd A.C. Scott, lived next to the church, was of Gothic design, very large, and catered for many of the weddings in the district. I did not often attend its services as my allegiance was to St Alban's but, on Saints' days, we were sometimes taken to the parish church with school parties.

There were also the church of St John the Evangelist on the Iffley Road served by the priests of the Society of St John the Evangelist (SSJE), or the Cowley Fathers as they were known; several free churches, and such establishments as the 'Good Shepherd Mission' (formerly the Salvation Army Hall) in Pembroke Street (now Rectory Road), supervised by Father P.G. Latham (later to become vicar of Sandford-on-Thames), and the Mission House of SS Mary and John at No. 14, Magdalen Road. The Mission House was worked by the Community of St John the Baptist and the sisters who lived there would attend, at any time, cases of sickness or distress or, by way of the Relief Committee, administer to the poor and needy.

Divine service was occasionally conducted in the Bartlemas chapel (dedication St Bartholomew), also used as a retreat, situated in a large meadow on the north side of the Cowley Road, a little beyond Magdalen Road. This restored chapel was once part of the hospital of St Bartholomew, now no longer in existence, but at one time a refuge for lepers, founded by Henry I.

At 52 St Clement's, Oxford, a church 'Rambler's Rest', was provided by the League of Our Father:

> It is for Men on the Road, who will always, every afternoon, from three to five-thirty, find a welcome there.
>
> The only material benefits are a cup of tea and a scone, (the strict rule of the League being that no money may be given away) and a fire to warm them, but that it is greatly appreciated by these poor men,

St Clement's, Oxford, with the Victoria drinking fountain, around 1910

who are the greater number ex-soldiers, is shown by the fact that during the year ending last September (1922) nearly seven thousand passed through it.

So did the church attempt to deal with both the moral and physical problems of those days.

However, the social side of church membership was not overlooked. The church hall next to the vicarage in Cowley Road provided amenities throughout the week for the guilds of St Mary and St Agnes, a boys' club, a girls' club, the Band of Hope, Church Lads' Brigade Cadets, men's guild, Mothers' Union, churchwomen's club and working party, and many other organizations.

The Revd A.C. Scott, vicar from 1910 to 1923 was a very popular man by reason of 'his kindly and genial disposition and general courtesy', and a study of his letters in the monthly magazine reveals that he also had a great sense of humour. During his incumbency money for church upkeep was a constant problem:

> Two words about money. We are putting up electric lights in the two gas lamps in the churchyard. It will cost eleven pounds.
> 'That is more than we can afford', said our Treasurer.
> 'All right,' I answered, 'I will be responsible.'

Will you all help? It will save many a broken head, perhaps your own! It won't be half as hard to give me one pound as to nurse a broken head.

Even this improved lighting must have been quite inadequate, for the graveyard surrounding the church was large and its main path led past the church through gravestones to an exit overhung with trees, which opened into Magdalen Road. I often used this route as a short cut during daytime, but could not face the walk through the memorial stones when night fell and cast menacing shadows on the pathway before me; at such times I took the longer walk along Cowley Road past the comforting light of the University Arms.

The difficulties of the times were reflected in the vicar's letter of January 1921: 'I wish you all a very happy New Year. We enter it hopeful that things will mend, that the year will see prices come down, and work found for our men.'

Still troubled in March 1921, he wrote: 'What with income tax and rates etc., etc., we don't know where we are,' and hopefully, 'If everyone will help, we shall save a few of the churchwardens' heads from turning grey, to say nothing of the vicar's.'

Evidently reeling under the strain of these problems he states in a later letter:

The University and City Arms in about 1910

I have lost my umbrella! and it is the only one I possess. Will those at whose houses I have called be so very kind as to look and see if they have an umbrella in their stand that they do not recognise.

He was not alone in his dilemma. The church choir fund seemed almost permanently on the verge of bankruptcy. Only the cheery spirit of its treasurer seems to have kept the choir in existence at all:

As I am not allowed by law to manufacture treasury notes and the manufacture of artificial diamonds is impossible, it is useless for me to try and save this fund by these methods, so I am resolved to hold the LAST whist drive, May 15th, 1920, and hope for support.

He backed up this appeal with the following notice:

The Church choir fund is like Waterloo Bridge – SINKING!
Wellington saved Europe in 1815.
Will our parish save this fund on the 15th?

The crisis must have been temporarily overcome, but in the following year he wrote: 'This fund, like the June weather, experienced a drought, there being no cash to acknowledge. The treasurer is now sowing seed of forget-me-not, with the hope of a good harvest in the autumn.'

By March 1926, the choir fund had benefited from sundry donations, the sale of a richly decorated ice cake which realized 12s., and six pounds of Turkish Delight, realizing 13s. 5d. but, sadly, these sums were not enough to ensure solvency and the parish magazine of July 1926 announced with regret the treasurer's resignation.

There was in existence a free-will offering fund which experienced similar difficulties, but its treasurer was more caustic in his approach: 'Many of those who undertook to make regular contributions are still alive, but some have forgotten to continue paying them.'

Despite these setbacks, the social life of the parish flourished:

On June 27th 1921 at 10.45 a.m., there was a wonderful sight in Magdalen Road! Four heavily laden charabancs started from the Mission House amid good wishes of friends and neighbours, and those of us who were fortunate enough to have secured places on them went off for a day's outing. With dignity we left the outskirts of the parish and passed through Littlemore – then Sandford, with its church standing still and its vicar running about, on through Nuneham, past the glorious Abbey of Dorchester.

At Windsor, some did one thing, some did another. Some called on the King, but did not find him in, so they went to the top of the tower instead to look at the view he looks at. Some looked at his throne, some at his horses, others at his carpet, and whatever it was they saw it gave them an excellent appetite for the gorgeous tea provided.

On 4 July 1922, there was a parish outing which was something of a washout: 'From here (Newbury) to Winchester, the beauty of the drive over the Downs was lost as the rain sheets had to be brought into use', but the catechism outing in August 1924 was a happier affair: 'There was paddling in the river, climbing trees, slipping about in the mud where we disembarked and embarked, and there was the entertaining game of losing hats, coats and shoes.'

Attached to the church was the 2nd Oxford Troop of Boy Scouts, who on 5 August 1923, set off for their annual camp, this time to Swanage in Dorset.

The sea was of course the primary attraction, only four boys (out of thirty-three) having been to the seaside before. They went on it by steamer to Bournemouth, in it and under it to bathe at every opportunity, in fact, not a few swallowed some of it in ecstasy!

but:

. . . who was the scout who wrote six letters home in the hope of raising funds to be spent in the canteen? – which contained anything from 'dreamy Daniels' (bars of toffee) to safety pins (in lieu of buttons). Evidently one scout did not think it worth while to waste much time in writing home, for his epistolary effort was condensed thus:

'S.O.S., L.S.D., R.S.V.P.'

Not to be outdone, the wolf cubs went to camp at Nuneham Park:

Somehow or other, the kit was placed aboard (the lorry) and we on top of it and away we went with the trek-cart rolling merrily behind, its two wheels kept in position by two clothes-pegs borrowed from the vicarage.

Parishioners, both young and old, also participated in the more serious aspects of church life. In 1924, during the Year of Prayer organized by the Anglo-Catholic Congress Committee, a Fiery Cross procession provided Oxford with a sight to remember, as noted in the parish magazine:

This parish is to have the honour of beginning, and the parish church and St Alban's are responsible for the twenty-four hours beginning at midnight on the 18th, including the whole of Sunday, October 19th. At 9.30 p.m. on Saturday the 18th, the parish clergy and priests of the Society of St John the Evangelist will receive the Fiery Cross at our end of Magdalen Bridge and will bring it in procession to the parish church. All parishioners who can do so are asked to be there and to follow in the procession.

On October 19th, the Fiery Cross will be at the parish church. A watch will be kept for twenty-four hours.

The vicar was well pleased:

I think everyone agrees as to the dignity and impressiveness of the Fiery Cross procession. It was really wonderful to watch the other procession with its great crowd coming across Magdalen Bridge to us at the Plain. And those who were in that procession have told me of the wonderful effect upon them when they saw our procession and crowd drawn up and waiting for them. I think what I noticed most was the quiet reverence shown everywhere by the spectators.

From the foregoing it will be seen that the church played a great part in our lives, both morally and socially, for it was a very active institution and in 1926, bearing in mind the rapidly increasing population, was very much aware of the work which lay ahead: 'There will be a great deal to be done in preparation for new parishes in this part of Oxford.'

# CHAPTER FOURTEEN

# THE RIVER THAMES

If the possibility of change and expansion agitated the minds of those responsible, it scarcely rippled the smooth surface of the River Thames which flows through the county of Oxfordshire; and living, as we were, in close proximity to the river, it naturally followed that we concerned ourselves greatly with the attractions of this waterway. From Folly Bridge the river ran cool and dark and in its depths could be seen darting fish and clusters of green reeds which bent at right angles as they reached the surface of the water, along which they then lay, pointing the way to Iffley Lock. This stretch of water is called the Isis, edged on its southern bank by a dusty white towpath, and its northern bank, from Folly Bridge to where the Cherwell joins the main river, was lined with college houseboats or barges. These picturesque craft moored under the red-flowering may and chestnut trees of Christchurch Meadow, were the scene of much activity in early spring. Paintwork was redecorated, carved emblems and figureheads were recoloured and gilded, and flags and bunting strung along the upper decks. All this was in preparation for the 'Eights', the inter-college boat races held during May of each year; a six-night series of bumping races beginning on a Thursday and ending on the following Wednesday. About thirty-four boats, each representing a college, were involved, rowing in three divisions at four, five and six o'clock. Because of the narrowness of the river, the boats, each holding eight brawny oarsmen and one diminutive cox, started one behind the other with a space of about two boat lengths between the stern of one boat and the prow of the next; the order being determined by the position in which they had finished the previous year. Excepting the leader, the aim of each boat was to draw close enough to touch some part of the boat immediately preceding and so effect a bump. When this was achieved, the cox of the bumped boat was obliged to signal by raising his arm and both boats then retired from that race. The following day, the boat which had been bumped took its place to the rear of the boat which had caused its demotion. It was also the cox's job to urge, encourage and verbally lambast his crew with such injunctions as 'paddle', 'look ahead', and finally, to the

'Eights Week' at Oxford in 1922

relief of the weary men, 'easy all'. He alone could see where he was going; his crew, concentrating on rowing, saw nothing more than the straining shoulder muscles of the man in front. The first boat in any division had, of course, merely to concentrate on keeping its stern well clear of the challengers in hot pursuit, and any boat which completed the course without either bumping or being bumped was said to have 'rowed over'.

This event was seen at its best if the weather was fine, for then families and friends of the crews were privileged to sit out on the top deck of the barge or on the cushioned seats of the saloon below, and the brightly coloured dresses of ladies, their big floral hats secured by veiling, the gaily striped blazers and straw boaters of the men supporters, and the fluttering flags and streamers, formed a gay tableau against a back-cloth of green foliage.

College servants did duty on the barges, serving innumerable cups of tea, ices and plates of fruit and cream as the crews set off for the starting point at Iffley. From the landing stage, they lowered themselves one by one into the frail shell, held in position by the cox; they adjusted their feet on the stretchers and tested their sliding seats, and then, if all was in order, the boat was pushed out and rowed leisurely down to Iffley amid cheers and cries of 'good luck' from the well-wishers.

Hugging the towing path side of the river were many punts; their occupants in varied attire – collars, ties, best suits, jackets, waistcoats, straw hats, caps and bowlers – were in holiday mood and undeterred by the noise and occasional cry of 'man overboard' were determined to see a fine finish. For their amusement, while the crews were making their way to the starting point, a band of singers of ragtime music performed to the accompaniment of banjo playing and appreciation of their efforts was sought by means of a collecting bag at the end of a long pole which was held out over the clustered punts and waggled invitingly.

Groups of spectators thronged the towpath for the entire length of the course, particularly for the six o'clock race. Men hurried home from work to partake of a quick cup of tea and a sandwich before hurrying down to the river, meeting on their way more fortunate friends who had attended

'Eights Week' on the river in 1920s

the earlier races, exchanging in passing enquiries as to the progress of the various eights. This happened in our house; father was given no peace until we were on our way, for we were never allowed on the towpath alone during Eights Week because of the rough and tumble of excited crowds. Arriving at the riverside, we sat down on the tufted grassy bank and waited with keen anticipation.

Meanwhile, at Iffley, the boats had been lined up in order and the sound of the five-minute starting gun brought everyone to their feet; a few moments of tension, then the one-minute starting gun was heard, after which the boats set off. Then babel broke out on the towpath: college runners, firing guns wildly, tore along the path, some on foot, others on bicycles, urging on their favoured boat, cheering a 'bump' and shouting hoarsely through megaphone or cupped hands. With complete disregard for spectators, they traversed the distance to the winning post, paying more attention to the direction of the skimming boats than to the direction of their own transport. On the final day of this exhausting display, arriving at the winning post, they flung themselves into the water and swam across to their barge amid the firing of many pistols.

To round off this event, a college whose crew had distinguished itself by becoming 'head of river' or had finished among the first three, or perhaps achieved six bumps during the races, often voted to give a 'bump' supper in celebration. These were great occasions for those privileged to attend and were followed by dancing, bonfires, on which an old boat was sometimes burned, and general larking about.

(During the General Strike of 1926, many members of college crews, having volunteered for national service, were called up and practice for the racing had to be abandoned.)

Enjoyable though these events were they had less attraction for me than one in which I could participate and I gained greater pleasure in paddling along the shady Cherwell when my parents decided to hire a punt for a Sunday trip. Punting was a popular pastime and in great evidence at weekends and on Thursday afternoons (Thursday was early closing day). Hire of such a craft for one afternoon and evening cost about 10s. but many people rented these boats for a week, in which case, in addition to camping equipment, the boat was fitted with several iron hoops over which, at night, a green canvas cover could be stretched.

One could follow this tributary of the Thames upstream through Christchurch Meadow, under the stone bridge of Magdalen, past Angel Meadow and Addison's Walk, finally coming to a halt at the rollers. At this point there was, and still is, a bathing-place called 'Parsons' Pleasure', for the use of men only, where nude bathing was allowed. Consequently, ladies were obliged to disembark and walk a short distance to a landing stage at the far end of the bathing-place, from whence they were collected by their escorts, who were permitted to take their boats through the swimming area. From then on the river ran through overhanging willows and flowering trees of the University Parks, later reaching the more open fields of Marston where the ragged robin grew and along the banks of which it was possible to tie up and picnic, or to swim.

However, this stretch of river was mostly frequented by experienced swimmers and we preferred to swim at the Long Bridges bathing-place. This was reached from our house by crossing the Iffley Road, walking down Fairacres Road, turning right into Parker Street and Warwick Street, then left down Bedford Street which led to Meadow Lane and a cinder track, at the bottom of which lay the free ferry across the Thames. The fields surrounding this track flooded during the winter months but the soggy earth was greatly appreciated by the animals which inhabited a nearby pig-farm. (Later an orchard was cut through, giving direct access from Fairacres Road to Meadow Lane, which considerably shortened the journey.)

Near to the ferry lay two small islands, the Great and Little Kidneys – 'Ketneys' in the fourteenth century – separated from the mainland by a backwater. These islands were a favoured spot for campers and for most of the summer the banks would be lined with bell tents, each in its roped enclosure, and identified from its neighbour by an inscribed name-board, such as 'Krushen Villa' or 'Seldom Inn'.

The only means of crossing the river between Folly Bridge and Iffley Lock was by private craft or by the ferry. The ferry-boat, punted across the river in leisurely peace in the cool of early morning, was besieged by a seething, pushing queue of children in the heat of a summer afternoon, so that the ferryman needed all his wits to control both them and his craft; but Tom Rose knew well how to handle both children and boats so that, as far as I am aware, these trips were undertaken without mishap.

'Enough', he would say, and push off from the bank, yet still the more daring would leap the widening gap, landing in a heap in the already well-loaded boat. Miraculously, that flat-bottomed craft survived the onslaught and I do not remember that it ever sank! Approaching the opposite shore the impatient few, having wormed their way to the front of the boat during its short journey, leapt the rapidly closing space and, landing on the crumbling bank of the towpath, sped along to the bathing-place, a distance of about two fields. During the 'Eights', the ferryman would time his trips across the river to fit in between the races – no mean achievement. One wonders what he would think of the Donnington Bridge which now spans the river so near to the scene of his labour.

At Long Bridges, segregation of the sexes was in force so that I usually went swimming with a girl friend and my brother with his friends. The first

Tom Rose, the ferryman

path across the field led to the 'boys' and the girls, a little further on, crossed a bridge, walked along a willow-lined path and into a large corrugated-iron enclosure. The water in this enclosure came straight from the river and the mind boggles at the thought of the pollution which must have been swallowed by learners in their first wallowing endeavours to swim. On the right as one entered were two long sheds fronted by canvas sheets, and in between these sheds, a row of little huts for the use of older ladies. At the end of the enclosure was another high corrugated-iron fence behind which lay the 'boys', the small door giving entrance to which was kept securely locked by an attendant, for, so it was whispered to me by a shocked girl friend, the boys undressed in sheds without a canvas screen and were free to swim in a state of nudity. Nothing, we decided, could be more disgraceful than this! To the right of the small door hung a large brass bell under which was a notice: 'In case of emergency, ring bell and unbolt door', but, to my knowledge, the bell was never rung.

The swimming area was divided into two depths by a narrow catwalk. In the shallow end struggled the beginners, supported by water wings, tin bottles strapped to their backs or on a belt suspended from a long pole and held by an instructor, while in the deep end there were diving boards for the more experienced. The attendant's hut daily displayed the temperature of the water and from this hut it was possible to hire a costume for a few pence. Costumes were usually made of black or navy cotton material, one-piece, with short sleeves and legs which reached to one's knees. During the hot summer days these costumes were in great demand, so that it frequently occurred that on applying to rent such a garment one was handed a wet, soggy, bundle discarded by an earlier swimmer, and getting into this was quite an uncomfortable experience.

A child could spend many hours at Long Bridges, coughing and spluttering through the test of ten yards and progressing up to a life-saving medallion. Each test passed entitled the swimmer to sew a two-inch strip of white tape on the front of his or her costume, each succeeding piece crossing the other like a star, finishing with a button in the centre, but with the medallion went an embroidered badge, worn with much pride.

During the winter months, we were taken swimming in school parties to the heated baths in Merton Street. There were several changing cubicles, before which was a wide corridor and here, with a partner, we practised our strokes, one child lying face downwards on a low padded stool, ankles grasped by the other, who then manipulated the legs in frog-like motion in unison with the would-be swimmer's arm movements. From the first we were taught the orthodox breaststroke and after turn and turn about at this practice were allowed into the shallow end of the baths. The water, clear and green, was inviting enough but the echoing noise of screams and

The Merton Street baths used by the author in the 1920s

laughter was shattering and off-putting to the row of shivering, long-costumed young children who stood, bathing caps pulled down to the eyebrows, on the tiled surround awaiting instructions to jump in: for a jump it had to be – we were not allowed to lower ourselves cautiously down from the steps. The baths were ten yards wide by twenty-five yards long, convenient for tests, so we knew that our first goal lay just across the baths and great was the thrill of success when after many futile attempts we fought our way over to that distant shore. When this was perfected there was the challenge of the deep end by diving boards, where one leapt gaily in, and it was probably sheer fright at finding no support beneath our feet which drove us on and on to the safety of the shallow end.

No doubt Merton baths, with the water reeking of antiseptic, was a much more hygienic place to swim, but, somehow, I preferred the shadowy depths of Long Bridges bathing-place; there, sharing the water with the reeds and an occasional eel, I felt at home.

The same stretch of river from which water flowed into the bathing-place was also favoured by steamers and launches. These, starting from Salter's boat-house at Folly Bridge, were popular for Sunday school outings in the summer and provided a child had sufficient attendance stamps on a card he or she was eligible for this annual junketing. Assembling at an

A steamer outing at Abingdon of the sort that the author went on

appointed spot, we walked to the wharf near the free ferry, known locally as Oxford docks, where we boarded a waiting steamer; this was a great thrill, to be afloat on what after all to us was a craft with the proportions of a sea-going liner! After the first excitement of casting off, we were out of our seats and swarming all over the boat. The captain was, fortunately, good tempered, having no doubt encountered the like before, so that apart from keeping a wary eye to see that no one fell overboard, he allowed us a free run of the vessel. The cabin was a great attraction; within minutes of setting off there would be booming business at the snack bar for lemonade and crisps; then, refreshed, up we would go on the top deck again to comment on the green fields and locks through which the steamer sailed. To pass under low bridges it was sometimes necessary to lower the hinged main funnel: then, for those sitting to the rear, it was a case of 'eyes down', to avoid the black smuts which blew from its interior.

At last we reached our destination – Nuneham Park. This was the home of Lord Harcourt who often allowed the use of his grounds, where peacocks and emus freely roamed, for such occasions as this. Disembarking at a landing stage and racing up a slope, we came to a parkland which seemed to stretch endlessly before us and on this expanse games and sports had been organized, after which both children and helpers repaired to the long trestle tables set out on the grass, for refreshments of tea, squash and thick wads of fruit slab cake, before returning to the steamer for the homeward trip. Outings were also arranged to Day's Lock and Wittenham Clumps, and for some children this was their only holiday of the year, and it was enjoyed to the full.

It must, however, have been something of an exhausting ordeal for the organizers as will be seen from the following extract from the parish magazine about one such trip:

About three hundred children assembled on July 6th, 1921 at the schools. Outside the gate was a barrow with ice creams. We embarked at the usual landing stage on two Thames liners – 'Queen of England' and 'Oxford'. All the boys and girls and the greater part of St Alban's girls in the larger steamer, and thereby hangs a tale! The large number of children, fortified with ice creams and carrying packets of food for lunch, weighed down the poor old steamer so much that we knocked against the bottom of the river and once or twice stuck fast for a minute or so.

This was partly due to the shallowness of the water and partly to what was alluded to above. (This is proved by the fact that the captain of the steamer, having seen the beautiful tea provided and the appetites of the children, absolutely refused to take so many back and a lot more were bundled into the ladies' boat. With the large boat thus lightened, and with the organist driving everyone towards the bow at the shallow parts, we got back in safety before midnight. Casualties – no children, but one coat overboard!)

Father Handover sat in the bow ready to charm with his voice any fierce bird or fish that might try to impede our progress. The organist was here, there and everywhere. The vicar and sacristan, on arriving, might have been seen at the pump with a pail, a piece of soap and a towel, many others might have been seen at the top of the Clumps.

And again in July 1922:

The girls went off from the 'Parish quay' at ten-thirty looking ever so nice, with bright faces and coloured hats, yellow, pink and all sorts of colours! The boys started from the school at eleven-thirty and walked to Iffley lock where they waited for the return of the steamer. We all enjoyed the voyage to Nuneham and, of course, none of the boys were sea-sick! We never heard the result of the girls' voyage – women do not generally talk about their little pains and sorrows. At Nuneham we had a great time. Lots of boys and girls tried to break their necks or their backs by running up and down what they called sandhills, but we expect the parents, when they saw the nether parts of the boys' garments, called them mad.

In those days the cost of hire of a steamer to Day's lock was 10 gns., and for most treats children were charged in accordance with their Sunday school attendance.

Those who have never missed will go free; those who have put in three-quarters of the attendance will have to pay sixpence; those who have put in half of the attendances must pay ninepence, and all who have done less than that, one shilling.

Further particulars will be given out in church and all questions (if they are not silly ones) will be answered.

Shorter river trips were available from Folly Bridge to Iffley lock and from here it was possible to walk to the attractive village of Iffley. (According to Henry Taunt, renowned photographer and local historian of the Victorian era, the earliest mention of this village occurs in the *Chronicles of Abingdon 941–6* as 'Gifteleia' which may be rendered as 'the field of gifts'.)

Two small bridges gave safe access over the weirs where the water swirled powerfully around the weir supports in deep, green swathes, cascading down to a lower depth of dancing, sparkling foam. Secretly, I was afraid of the weir and of the cruel sweep of water, so I would take care to hold tightly to the bridge railings as I crossed.

At the end of the second bridge was a toll-gate through which one was permitted to pass on payment of a halfpenny. The toll-house was the property of an Oxford college and had been in existence for many years, but it was resented by local residents, some of whom marched boldly past the outstretched hand of the toll-gate keeper with the one word 'Iffley', as though it were a magic password. Needless to say, it was not long before small boys began to copy this manoeuvre, though meeting with less success. The toll-gate also caused annoyance to visitors: Mr Taunt records that a member of one party of touring Americans when asked for the toll protested: 'Pay a toll! pay a toll! What for? To come over a little wooden bridge; we never heard of such an imposition.'

The toll-gate at Iffley lock

But the keeper was adamant, the toll was paid, and the disgruntled party moved on with a final question: 'And pray, what do you do with the money you take?' which elicited the sharp reply: 'We give it away in prizes to people who mind their own business.'

The power of the toll extended beyond the living; a coffin would not be allowed through the gate, for this, it was said, would have established a right of way; so although mourners were allowed through, the coffin would be taken by boat to another spot on the Iffley shore and from thence to the nearby church. This curious situation arose in 1926 and was reported in the *Oxford Times*, which prompted a reader to write: 'I am under the impression that our forefathers got over such difficulties by inserting in the stile or gate that barred their progress, three 'black pins', and by so doing paid for the accommodation and raised no question of right.'

Very near to the toll-gate, a small entrance in a wall led to the site of the Iffley mill which, sadly, was destroyed by fire on 20 May 1908. From here the uneven stony lane rose sharply to the road which ran through the village. At the top of this lane stood a large house with a magnificent bay window overlooking the lock; indeed, the village included several fine houses and attractive cottages, a school with a thatched roof and a wall-stone inscribed 'Iffley Parochial School MDCCCXXXVIII', and a Norman

Iffley Mill after the disastrous fire in 1908

church dating probably about 1160. To the left of the church a stiled lane led through cornfields to Littlemore and this was a favourite walk with courting couples. Iffley was a delightful village: in the afternoon one could wander through its sunlit ways, savouring its peace and serenity without meeting a soul; past the fine elm tree standing on a grassy mound, near to which once stood the village stocks, too soon reaching its end, where the narrow road turned left and became Iffley Turn, an area of magnificent chestnut trees where we searched among the fallen leaves for glossy brown conkers, or in nearby Sandy Lane for beechnuts. The Turn was also the terminus where one waited, sitting on a seat of cold iron piping, for the city bus.

# CHAPTER FIFTEEN

# FAIRS AND FIREWORKS

In striking contrast to the tranquillity of Iffley village, a noisy event in the wide street of St Giles annually shatters the peace of the city – the fair!

The people of Oxford have enjoyed many fairs in their time. There is documented record of St Frideswide's Fair in 1122, and Gloucester Green Fair was known to have existed in 1601, but this was abolished in 1915. A large fair was still held in St Clement's around 1900 on the Thursday before Michaelmas, but by the early 1920s this had greatly diminished in size, consisting merely of one or two children's roundabouts situated on the cobbled area in front of the Black Horse Inn; so that at this time, the only fair of any consequence existing in Oxford was St Giles's Fair, to which people came from near and far.

St Giles's Faier.
Us cums frum Head'nton Quaary, an' sum frum Shotover Hill,
An' sum on us cums fru' Whaately, an' sum all th' way fru' Brill,
Fru' Milton an' fru' 'Aasely, frum Stad'am an' Talmage Stoke,
Frum out of th' Otmoor country, an' t'others they cums from Noke;
We all on us cums to Auxford, brought in by th'ould gray mare,
'Tis only wunce a year us cums, an' that's to St. Giles Faier.

Us meets sum pals frum Yarnton, sum more from Norligh too,
From Blechinton an' Chalton, where they cuts 'um half-a-two,
An' Chalberie an' 'Ooten, from Wesson-on-th'-Green,
An' sum from Coate and Climbly, the only time they're seen;
We all on us rides to Auxford, behind o' th'ould gray mare,
'Tis only wunce a year us cums, an' that's to St. Giles' Faier.

An' then us sees old Boozer, as cums from Witney town,
But you maunt chaff him either, or much about he'll fraown,
An' Jack what hails fru' Bampton, an' Joe what cums fru' Leaow,★

They all hev brought thur lasses, but how I dosen't kneaw;
Somehow um rides to Auxford, behind o' th'ould gray mare,
'Tis only wunce a year um cums, an' that's to St. Giles' Faier.

Us mixes in the dancing, Bor-bye us likes it well,
An' goes to see th'helephant, by gorms, ain't he a swell,
Us to th' 'Harse an' Jockey' goes in to have some yale,
An' then us larks about th'faier until it all gets stale;
When whoam us all goes from Auxford, behind o' th'ould gray mare,
'Tis only wunce a year, ye kneaw, us cums to St. Giles' Faier.

★Well sur, I belave as how they spells un Lew, but us calls un Leaow fur short.

The above is an Oxfordshire folklore ditty, extracted from the notes of Henry Taunt. To him also I am indebted for the following observation on the history of the fair: 'St Giles' Fair is one of the last survivals of the wakes or fairs which belonged to many of the religious houses. This is held in the manor of Walton which once belonged to Godstow Nunnery.'

According to a pamphlet, 'Fairs' by R.W. Muncey, the earliest reference

Crowds at St Giles' fair in the 1920s

to St Giles' Wake is 1625, and Sally Alexander's book *St Giles' Fair 1830–1914* states: 'St Giles' was not in origin a fair at all but a wake, a local parish feast' and: 'St Giles' is not an ancient chartered fair and little is known about it before the nineteenth century'.

To allow children to attend the fair which was held on the first Monday and Tuesday following the first clear Sunday in September, the school summer holidays were for five weeks and two days. The event took place (and still does) in St Giles', a wide thoroughfare in the city centre and necessitated the closure of this road to through traffic. However, the police would not allow fair vehicles in the area until very early on Monday morning, so that it became a family tradition to rise in the misty dawn and, with father, cycle into the town to watch the caravans come in.

In the week previous to the fair, the showmen had gathered in outlying fields or on waste ground so that no time should be lost on the morning when entry to Oxford was permitted, and promptly at 4 a.m. they trundled their vehicles into St Giles'. From then on all was hustle, and the speed and mechanical skill of these men of little schooling was indeed a sight to behold. Sweating, straining, they unpacked the gaudily painted sections of wood and metal; they slotted, hammered and screwed until suddenly, there was a roundabout, to which a hissing belching steam-engine soon gave life and by eight o'clock the fair was attracting its first customers. There was competition amongst the showmen as to whose equipment should be first in motion and for many years this honour went to the Nicholls family.

Despite the lack of education, the showmen were by nature a very astute race. Whole families were involved, the Bucklands, Studts, Birds, Thurstons and Wilsons to mention a few. They lived carefully and their combined efforts were chiefly concentrated on the maintenance of their equipment, for to have a machine standing idle meant loss of money. The senior member of a family, though perhaps too old for active work, nevertheless appeared to control the joint finances. One old lady, I remember, would sit all day on the steps of her caravan watching the revolutions of her machines; it was said she could estimate almost to a penny the takings for each ride, so that at the day's end she had a pretty good idea of how much money should be tipped onto her table for counting. With her individual method of 'figgerin', what need had she of multiplication tables!

The most popular roundabout was the 'big horses'. These were magnificent beasts arranged three deep on a circular platform. As this platform revolved the horses went up and down and the sensation, particularly on the outside steeds, could be quite exhilarating. Prices were lower in the morning so my friends and I would take our rides early and save the sideshows for the afternoon, for we had saved throughout the year for this event, so the money was spent with great care. In the writing bureau of my home

The gallopers at St Giles' fair in the 1920s

stood three red money boxes fashioned as postal pillar boxes, with a large slit near the top lid on which was scratched the initial of its owner. Into this receptacle, during the year, we slipped our pennies, halfpennies and occasionally a bright half-crown, and on the day prior to the fair the boxes were turned upside down and with the aid of a large knife placed in the slit, we extracted our savings and divided the total into two piles, one for the Monday fair, one for Tuesday. I seem to recall that my hoard worked out at about 5s. per day, but as rides cost a few pence only, it was possible to do quite a lot with this allowance.

Other roundabouts were the chairaplanes, where small seats suspended by chains from a circular ceiling swung out above the heads of the crowd as the machine gathered momentum, and the Wältzer, in which about a dozen tub-like seats, secured to a revolving platform, themselves revolved in spasmodic movements, so that the riders were thrown left and right as well as round and round. It was impossible to tell if the screams issuing from these contraptions were of delight or fear, but once on board there was no getting off and, when the revolutions stopped and the passengers leapt or staggered off according to their physical ability, there was certainly no lack of replacements and little delay before the motion resumed. The Cakewalk consisted of two long corridors In and Out, with the floor constantly moving up and down and backwards and forwards. The pressure of those behind made some kind of erratic forward progress necessary if one was ever to get off.

Mostly these old favourites occupied the same site each year; even today the Mat tower still rises next to the war memorial. Sliding on a mat down the track encircling the tower soon became fairly tame and we preferred to patronize the Switchback. Here, the circular platform was so constructed that carriages, each holding about twelve persons and running on a track at its perimeter, rose and fell at great speed and it was necessary to hold on very tightly if one was not to be thrown out. These carriages had red plush seats and were of striking design, showily painted in bright colours with gold trimmings. Each had a figurehead of what appeared to be a prehistoric monster with gaping jaws exposing a fiery red tongue and stark, white fangs: this creature would appear to pause at the height of a slope, then descend with a swoop as if to devour any small person in its path. Mercifully, the limitations of the track diverted this beast so that it swept harmlessly out of sight.

The rich tone of the music which accompanied these mad revolutions resulted from feeding long, perforated rolls of parchment into the gilded mechanical organ, the spectacular appearance of which was enhanced by puppet-like figures beating time with small batons. Mobile steam-engines generated power for the electrical supply to hundreds of light bulbs.

In addition to small roundabouts for children there were the sideshows and stalls: whelks, shrimps, toffee apples, rock, coconut ice, nougat, brandy snaps and Banbury cakes were all on sale. There were toy stalls of glassy-eyed dolls, and pink, blue and yellow teddy bears; fruit stalls, men selling cheap jewellery, watches, gold chains and bead necklaces. There were dart stalls offering prizes of gaudily painted vases, china dogs and glassware, and, for the young bloods of the town, shooting galleries where they might show off their skill.

Many people came specially to the fair to renew their household goods, and newlyweds to stock their homes. There were stalls selling Nottingham lace curtains and china and glass stalls from which it was possible to buy bargains if one was prepared to haggle good-humouredly with the vendor. Standing on a wooden box, regarding the crowd, he would begin:

Now ladies and gentlemen, I have here a lovely twelve-piece bone

TOFFEE APPLES

Toffee apples at the fair

china tea-set, rose-patterned, all intact, just the thing for you ladies to take afternoon tea; and what am I asking for this lovely tea-set? Not £3, which it is worth, not £2 15s. 0d., or even £2 10s. 0d!

His sharp eyes scanned the crowd looking for the first sign of acceptance before lowering his price. Finally amidst forecasts of his own bankruptcy he might sell it for £1 10s. 0d., leaving his assistant to wrap the goods and collect the cash while he harangued the crowd with details of his next 'give-away' offer. From this stall too, for a few pence, children could buy small china or glass ornaments as 'fairings' for their mothers.

For those who still had money there was 'Rolling the Penny' in which a penny was placed in a sloping wooden slot so that it ran down on to a circular table covered with numbered squares. Certain squares were coloured and these were lucky, entitling one to a prize if the coin settled clearly within.

In the centre of the fair, by the lamp-posts adorned with 'Beware Pickpockets' notices, stood the cheap-jacks selling lucky brooches, mascot dolls, balloons, streamers and ticklers. These last were cardboard handles with a horsehair switch favoured by the young men who used them to tickle the faces of the young girls among the crowd and they, while professing annoyance, secretly enjoyed the whole procedure.

For these young people the 'Wall of Death' was a prime attraction, where motor-cycles roared round and round a huge cylindrical structure at sufficient speed to mount its wall so that the machines were in a horizontal position at the peak of their momentum, and their dare-devil riders were the source of much envy and admiration.

Just after 1900 the arrival of the bioscope show had caused great excitement at the fair. Standing on a raised platform outside the tent, two cow-boys would cry and shout, firing their guns madly into the air in an effort to attract attention to this new wonder. These moving pictures, heralded by the magic lantern, were shown in a booth fitted up like a theatre, but by the 1920s these 'living pictures' had been promoted from the fairground to the picture palace.

Right at the end of the fair in Woodstock Road was a big show owned by Prince Samudi, who boasted such miraculous feats as sawing a woman in half. As he extolled the attractions of his performance, tempting his audi-ence, a small monkey on a long chain would descend from a pole and, min-gling with the crowd, collect pennies in an old tin cup.

There was always a tent manned by St John Ambulance Brigade and another for lost children, both pitched behind the walled area before St John's College, and nearby, a small tent representing a religious organization, a member of which would periodically reproach the crowd for its sinfulness and urge the rejection of self-indulgence. But the mood of the crowd appeared little affected by the warning of doom to come; maybe the orator's words were largely unheard, for the general din of music, screams, laughter and shouts of the stall-holders rose above all else.

In this area also was to be found a diminutive figure immaculately attired in frock-coat and top hat and attracting a large crowd. This was Jimmy Dingle, a local man, who in his lifetime raised a great deal of money for the Radcliffe Infirmary through such appeals as this.

Although often penniless long before the day ended, my companions and I would spin out the time until dusk, loath to leave this world of speed and excitement, its attraction now intensified by the glitter of lighted bulbs which flashed and reflected on the gilded metallic surfaces in a kaleidoscope of colour set against a darkening sky. As the pace of the machines appeared to increase, so did the cost of the rides, though it was suspected that they were of shorter duration; and the cries of vendors, their wares now illu-mined by paraffin flares, became more frenetic in an effort to be heard above the din. It mattered little to us that the surface of this usually stately thoroughfare was littered with paper wrappings, half-eaten sausages, or stained by squashed chips; such things were trivial in the maelstrom of delight and, as we walked home, albeit wearily, the fun of the day was still with us.

By 9 a.m. the following day it was difficult to believe such an event had taken place in the dignified street of St Giles'; for by then all fair equipment had disappeared; protective fencing around the war memorial had been dis-mantled; and the roadway had been swept and sprinkled with disinfectant. Traffic flowed freely again through this tree-lined street and only a child, pass-ing through on his way to school, might pause to note a patch of oil where the steam-boats had stood or remember the enchantment of the previous day.

After St Giles's Fair we would save what money came our way for the November the Fifth celebrations. Halfpenny bangers, grasshoppers, penny packets of sparklers and twopenny rockets were painstakingly purchased, stored in a box, fetched out, counted and examined, almost daily. Most of these treasures were bought from a nearby house which opened its front room in October of each year for the sale of such articles. The house was owned by a man and his sister rejoicing in the names of Digby and Marian, both well spoken and giving an impression of breeding somewhat above the level of our street. It was said that their mother was 'well connected' and that at one time their father had owned a theatre in Oxford, also that both children had spent much time travelling about the country, which probably accounted for the fact that neither had received much formal schooling. Their furniture certainly was of good quality, though neglected, and Digby would call at the baker's for a loaf of bread, attired in bowler hat and frock-coat as to the manner born. He was a man of spasmodic occupation, being in great demand at Christmas time as a ventriloquist and conjurer, a skill he no doubt acquired hanging around the wings of a theatre in his childhood days. Occasionally, in his more affluent periods, he would emerge as a developer, buying an individual plot of land and engaging a builder to erect a house on it which he then sold. He must have made a reasonable profit on these transactions for there were long periods when he did no work at all, yet his ego knew no bounds, and both he and his sister assumed a superior and disdainful manner towards their neighbours.

It was Marian who attended to the sale of fireworks. Seating her ample proportions behind a long table on which these explosive delights were exhibited, she appeared to show little interest in her task and even a tendency to nod off, but, let one child surreptitiously attempt to slide a banger or a grasshopper into his pocket and she would open one eye to say in a genteel tone: 'That'll be a penny dear!'

She would take the proffered cash and divide it into two boxes marked D and M, so that by the end of the day profits were equally divided between brother and sister without the tiresome task of calculation.

Having acquired the fireworks, we then set about making a guy and father would build a bonfire in the garden. Friends were invited in on the night to enjoy the fun, but never did time go so slowly. At the first sign of dusk we would pester father to start the proceedings, but were bade to be patient and not until it was dark enough would he begin. Then it was that we appreciated the reason: against the dark, dark sky our twopenny rockets zoomed heavenwards leaving behind a trail of gold; Roman candles sent up feathered trees of coloured lights, and Catherine wheels, pinned to the fence, whirled in concentric circles of purple, red and yellow, edged with flashing sparks. The bonfire flared and crackled as we fed it with twigs and old cardboard boxes saved over many weeks; flames licked greedily around the guy and slowly devoured his newspaper-stuffed body covered with father's old jacket and a child's woolly hat.

For one glorious hour the garden was lit by the fire's reflection: trees and fences stood out in black relief and large shadows rose and fell across the row of little houses. Neighbours' gardens were in a similar state to ours so that the whole area appeared to be in the throes of some devilish ceremony; an impression accentuated by the screams and shouts of those taking part. But gradually, the carefully hoarded supply of fireworks disappeared, the bonfire became merely a heap of red embers, and we trooped reluctantly indoors to refreshments of hot potatoes in jackets, cheese and cups of soup, leaving behind, under a pall of smoke, a garden dark and empty.

# CHAPTER SIXTEEN

# AROUND AND ABOUT

As we grew older we deserted street and garden and roamed further afield for amusement, often spending whole days with a group of friends picnicking on Shotover; a curious name, often attributed to a belief that it was a hill 'shot over' by Robin Hood or Oliver Cromwell; but records assert that 'it is now generally held that the name derives from the Old English – *sceot ofer,* a steep slope'. To reach this pleasant spot meant a walk of two or three miles, commencing through the rec. at the bottom of our street, out into the Cowley Road, turning east towards the Morris works, but leaving the main road at the Cowley Marsh, beyond which lay the golf links. Crossing the marsh we reached a sandy lane leading to Hollow Way, an area of heathland, and standing out starkly in these pastoral surroundings was Cowley Barracks, built in 1876. During the 1914–18 war, soldiers from this

A rural scene from Lye Hill in 1914 with Cowley Barracks in the background

establishment dug trenches and exercised themselves on the rec. and were often to be seen in the city during off-duty hours. At the end of Hollow Way the track veered left to Slade Common, bordered on one side by Magdalen Woods, a popular haunt of gypsies. Here they could park their caravans, graze the horses, festoon the bushes with washing and whittle away the hours making pegs of branches cut from nearby trees.

But our goal lay along a footpath turning right from the end of Hollow Way, on through open fields and scrub to Open Brasenose; this was really only the lower slopes of Shotover, but as by this time we were usually hot and tired, this was the spot chosen to set up camp. For we did not travel lightly; a mixed party of boys and girls, we were laden with bats and balls, sandwiches, fruit and lemonade, as though preparing for a siege. An added, though essential, encumbrance was the gramophone; one boy with the turntable, another with the records and a third with the horn slung under one armpit. I recall on one occasion a heated argument outside the Cowley Barracks when it was discovered that one member of the party had forgotten his allotted task, to bring the gramophone needles, and was sent back home for them, post haste!

Open Brasenose was an area dotted with clumps of yellow, prickly gorse and the grass streaked with narrow beaten tracks, threading through bracken, leading – who knew where? There were patches of woodland where

Brasenose Farm in 1916 with Shotover in the background

elm and oak combined in a leafy canopy over primrose, violet and wood anemone nestling at the boles; and the soil beneath our feet was springy with the decayed foliage of countless years. Dog-rose, nettle and bramble grew in unrestricted freedom, but scratches, stings and snagged clothing were an accepted hazard and did not detract from the fun of exploration or 'hide and seek'. The place was a delight of flat plains and hilly slopes which, swathed in bluebells, swept down from the woodland and wrapped themselves around little green valleys.

Fortunately this wooded expanse was very large and there were no houses in the vicinity so that we played rounders or generally larked about to our hearts' content to the blaring accompaniment of the good-tempered instrument; and meat pie or cheese sandwich never tasted so good as then, sitting astride a fallen tree or lolling in the rough grass in the sunshine and the fresh sweet air of the countryside.

But when the weather became too cold for picnics, my brother and I often walked to the town on Saturday mornings, a distance of about two miles, along the Iffley Road, past the running track to the Plain. In the

The Plain, Oxford, in 1922 where the author remembers a temperance stall was regularly to be seen

centre of the road where Iffley Road and Cowley Road met was a public convenience surrounded by ornate iron railings, and at the junction of Cowley Road and St Clement's a churchyard, its railings enclosing old gravestones leaning at all angles and, dominating this churchyard, a monument to the fallen of the South African war. Nearby, the Victoria drinking fountain, erected by the Morrell family in 1899, stood on the site of St Clement's toll-house. At the press of a button, fresh, sparkling water gushed forth above the ornamental step basins clustered around the centre of this structure, to be greedily gulped by hot schoolboys from half-spherical iron cups secured to the basins by chains. Encircling the base of the fountain were troughs, intended to assuage the thirst of passing horses, but which, in the past, had sometimes been used to cool off the more lively lads of the district. Near to the fountain and facing Magdalen College School stood a coffee cabin, a wooden vehicle, the side flap of which lifted up to form a canopy, revealing a counter, rows of thick white mugs and 'doorsteps' of bread and cheese. During cold weather, by means of a coke stove whose chimney protruded through the roof of the vehicle, supplies of hot steaming tea and coffee were brewed and the slopping cups slid onto the narrow counter where they were gratefully grasped by hands blue and trembling with cold. The cabin must have stood on this spot for many years for I recall my father telling me of the time, around the turn of the century, when, in company with other boys on mischief bent, he clambered up the rear of this cabin and placed an inverted tin can over the top of the chimney so that thick, black smoke blew back into the interior of the cabin causing the irate owner and his wife to retreat hurriedly. That may well have been one occasion when the horse troughs were put to another use!

Crossing Magdalen Bridge, with Magdalen School on our left partially hidden by lime trees, and on the far side of the bridge to the left, the entrance to the botanical gardens and Rose Lane leading to Christchurch Meadow, we passed on our right the tower of Magdalen College pointing gracefully to the sky.

The stateliness of High Street, flanked by university buildings, was not then greatly appreciated by us: this came later; our immediate goal and concern was the penny bazaar in St Ebbe's. This was a narrow shop with a long counter on the right as one entered, crammed with articles costing one penny: pencils, rubbers, kitchen implements and general household goods. It was here that I did most of my shopping for presents, decorations, dolls' furniture – a veritable Aladdin's cave.

My brother, on the other hand, being slightly more affluent than I, patronized Woolworth's Sixpenny store in Cornmarket Street, newly opened in 1925. Referred to among the younger generation as 'Woollies', it was probably the beginning of departmental stores in Oxford and on the morning of its opening, Norman rose early, breakfasted on a wad of bread and jam and set off for the town before the rest of the family was astir. His object and reward for this dedication was to be at the head of the queue and one of the first children to enter the new store. He had also achieved the doubtful distinction of being among the first patrons of the Super Cinema which opened in 1924.

Almost opposite Woolworth's stood Grimbly Hughes, a fascinating and exclusive grocery store which stocked spices and exotic foods from foreign countries in addition to more homely products, but all was presented with taste and served with politeness. One traversed the shop along narrow avenues between wooden crates of fruit and vegetables and a central counter stacked with boxes of crystallized fruit and other preserves. Even the counters which ran along either side of the shop were crammed with boxes, tins and packets, with an occasional aperture through which an assistant, standing behind the counter, peered encouragingly. All these stacked goods made the shop rather dark but this only added to the atmosphere of elegance and mystery.

Most shops in the town kept their electric lights burning until quite late in the evenings, so providing a glowing attraction for the lads and lasses of

Grimbly Hughes' Grocery shop in the Cornmarket, around 1924

the town. A square formed by Cornmarket Street, George Street, New Inn Hall Street, and Queen Street, was known as the 'Bunnyrun' and in the evenings young adolescents would parade round and round this square, exchanging flippant greetings or stopping in lighted shop doorways to further an acquaintance. My friends and I were too young to indulge in this activity, but we were, nevertheless, well aware of its existence.

A little further north, on the same side of the street as Grimbly Hughes' shop stood the Clarendon Hotel. The green and white painted façade of this building was attractive even to a child. Boxes of geraniums and lobelia lined its window sills in summer and from the front entrance, over the pavement, stretched a wrought-iron canopy, the corners of which were hung with baskets of like flowers. Near to the hotel was the Cadena, famed for its coffee and baking of bread and cakes; to enter its doors was to walk into a world of refinement. Sometimes, for a treat, my parents would take us to tea there. Seated at a small table covered with a spotless white cloth, we gazed rapturously at a tall silver cake stand on which reposed cream cakes, doughnuts and chocolate éclairs. (Rich pastries at this time cost about 2s. for a dozen and a really rich Dundee cake from 2s. 3d. to 7s. 6d.) To add to the dignity of the occasion a small orchestra of three ladies played classical

The Cornmarket in 1922 with the Clarendon Hotel on the left

music, conversation was low and controlled and the atmosphere such as to ensure our good behaviour.

The life of the city revolved around the crossroads at its centre – Carfax. On the north-west corner stood the tower of St Martin's church, the top of which was accessible from a spiral iron staircase, affording a fine view of the city roof-tops. On the north-east corner a bank, on the south-east a very old Oxford haberdasher, Wyatt's, and on the south-west, Boffin's cake shop, of half-timbered construction, which had a great reputation for its confectionery and, like the Cadena, was a popular meeting place for morning coffee. The western arm of the crossroads led down Queen Street and here, in a small shop, was situated the Oxford Wireless and Telephony Company. From here, such events as the Oxford and Cambridge Boat Race were broadcast publicly and those who did not possess a wireless set stood about in groups in the roadway anxious to take advantage of the medium. Travelling north from Carfax leaving the shops behind, one came to a division in St Giles': on the right, Banbury Road giving access to the university parks, and on the left Woodstock Road in which stood the Radcliffe Infirmary, whilst almost opposite the hospital entrance was a shabby building, home of a local repertory company later to find a more impressive home in Beaumont Street under the title 'Oxford Playhouse'.

When holidays allowed I liked to visit the cattle market, held on Wednesdays where the Gloucester Green bus station now is, and from here to wander across a hump-backed bridge which spanned the Oxford canal, to where Oxford Castle nestled, almost unnoticed, behind a green, grass mound, in New Road:

> Came Matilda to me in the twelfth century,
> For refuge from Stephen, who tried
> With might and main an entrance to gain,
> His armies I stoutly defied.
> I guarded her safely during his siege,
> Till provisions and arms running low,
> Under cover of night, with attendants in white,
> She slipped quietly away through the snow.
> I guarded your peace and I kept Oxford safe
> From peril, in times gone by.
> So have I not earned a thought or a glance
> From you who hurry nigh?

At the end of this road lay the Great Western Railway station and the London, Midland and Scottish Railway station.

After this journeying we were glad to take a bus home, travelling from

High Street, Oxford, in 1932 with a station bus and a Morris Minor van amongst the traffic

the railway station to the Magdalen Road terminus where the Regal cinema now stands, for three halfpence. In 1914, despite some opposition, motor buses had superseded the horse trams which had served Oxford so faithfully since 1881. The first bus company was run by W.R. Morris, later to become Lord Nuffield, and when, in the first instance, he found himself unable to obtain a licence to sell tickets on his vehicles, he arranged for local shops to do this, acting as his agents. One such shop was a small green-grocer next to the University Arms public house on the corner of Magdalen Road. Later, the City of Oxford Motor Services came to be accepted and began to expand. The buses, which were garaged overnight in Leopold Street, had solid tyres and were open topped with outside staircase and the seats of ribbed wood, painted yellow ochre, had a rubber apron suspended from the back for shelter during wet weather of the passengers seated behind. (During the 1914–18 war, these seats had been removed and the entire top deck was occupied by a gas-bag, refilled as necessary from a gas supply stand-pipe which was erected at the Magdalen Road terminus.) Bus tickets were of varying colour, price and shape and held by the conductor in a large piece of wood fitted with spring clips, from which they were extracted and punched with a small machine which emitted a bell-like sound. These tickets, when carelessly thrown down at bus-stops, were eagerly collected by Norman and sorted, the aim being to acquire a numbered sequence with the help of a swapping system among his friends.

In addition to the buses, more private cars were appearing on the roads, but in 1926 the city streets were still shared by many kinds of transport, sometimes with comical results according to the *Oxford Times* newspaper: 'One day this week a horse was seen warming its nose on the radiator of a car in Cornmarket Street. It was with considerable difficulty that the carter induced the animal to leave its "hot water bottle".'

# CHAPTER SEVENTEEN

# CHRISTMAS

With the advent of Christmas, all thought of roaming was abandoned. This was a time for home and family, and looking back over the years, my childhood memories of the season are of magic, colour and warmth.

Preparation for the event began some weeks ahead and meant a great deal of hard work in which the whole family was involved. Joyce and I were willing helpers in the kitchen, stoning raisins, cutting up candied peel and mixing the pudding which was then stirred by each member of the family in turn who were, at the same time, allowed to make a wish. A big fruit cake was baked and later iced and decorated with miniature figures of Father Christmas and his reindeer, and finally encircled with a coloured paper frill. One of the treats of all this activity, as far as Joyce and I were concerned, was that we were allowed to eat the raisins and sugar extracted from the candied peel, or to wipe the various basins and utensils clean with a small forefinger! Silver cutlery was extracted from wash-leather bags and cleaned with pink polish; the best dinner and tea services were fetched out from their boxes, washed, and stored in the larder until needed; wine glasses and big crystal bowls, used only at parties, were washed and polished so that they sparkled with colour and light.

In the few days before 25 December, we bought packets of coloured paper cut into strips and, with a big bowl of flour paste, made these strips into rings connecting into each other like a chain, and this was then strung back and forth across the room. Rows of dancing girls were cut from folded coloured paper and pinned along the draping of the mantelshelf, and bells, lanterns or angels, fashioned from coloured crêpe paper, hung on every available hook.

The hall ceiling was usually the place for a bunch of mistletoe, and ivy and holly which we collected from the hedgerows was lodged behind the many pictures. Father would bring home a big fir branch and this we planted in an old bucket covered with crêpe paper and placed in the front room, where it was later decorated with small candles set in tin holders, brightly coloured baubles, and some of the smaller presents.

We spent many hours on dark winter evenings making our presents for each other. Any attractive coloured pictures had previously been cut out from magazines and the largest of these were now mounted on stiff cardboard as calendars, at the bottom of which a small book calendar, purchased from Batten's for one penny, was suspended. Small pictures were stuck on folds of plain white paper and crayoned messages of greeting written within, and these were our Christmas cards which we sent to relatives and friends. Last minute Christmas shopping was usually done as a family and in the evening for the shops kept open very late at this season. The main shopping area in Cowley Road was lined with stores whose tinselled trappings glistened and sparkled in the fluttering gaslight. There seemed to be an abundance of everything: pyramids of fruit, crates of vegetables; and, above the poulterer's shop window, rows of plucked turkeys, geese and other fowl were suspended by their feet. Business would be brisk on Christmas Eve, for then shopkeepers reduced their prices in order to dispose of their goods before the holiday. All was bustle, and in my memory exciting! We mingled with other shoppers heavily laden with bulky parcels, Christmas trees and, here and there, a straw bag from which protruded, on one side the trussed feet and on the other the bored, dead face of a turkey.

Shopping completed and leaving the bright lights behind we walked home through the side streets dimly lit by gas lamps. Street lamps were ignited by a time-clock in the lantern, the ticking of which was clearly audible to anyone sitting on the kerb below, and periodically checked by a man who toured the area on a bicycle, one arm slung through the rungs of a short ladder. At each lamp-post he would dismount from his bicycle, place the ladder against an arm jutting out below the lantern, climb up, open the glass panel and wind the clock; this done he would clamber down again and collecting his ladder set off down the road to the next lamp. The jutting arm would be used on bus routes to accommodate a hanging sign 'Bus stop', in blue or red enamel, but in our street it was used as an anchor for ropes on which we could swing, or boys would shin up the lamp and, grasping this arm, swing out over the pavement. Needless to say, neither of these activities took place when the lamp-lighter was around. Spaced at intervals on alternate sides of the road, the lamps were of great significance to us, each being named after the nearest householder. Thus we would say: 'I'll meet you at Keep's lamp' or: 'I'll race you to Wood's lamp.'

There was obviously great affection for these lamps and distrust of anything new, for the *Oxford Times,* reporting on a meeting of parishioners of Cowley states:

The Cowley parishioners are of an economical turn of mind in regard to the lighting of the village. The choice lay between a two-penny rate

126

and gas and a fourpenny rate and electricity. The Chairman remarked that electric light was very nice but it was a luxury.

The light shed by the gas lamps was murky and confined itself to a circle around the standard, but they were friendly, none less so when, during the walk home on Christmas Eve, one came upon the Waits clustered around the lamp-post as if in a lighted cone, brass instruments winking to the accompaniment of lustily played carols. This was the true spirit of Christmas and we were glad to put down our parcels and, sitting on someone's front wall, join in the singing.

Continuing our homeward journey, we were then more than ready for bed and went willingly, after hanging a long, black woollen stocking on the bedpost. The thrill of finding that same stocking bulging with mysterious, crackling parcels on the following morning lasted for several years. Norman would bring his gifts into our room and we all sat on the bed surrounded by parcels, apples, oranges, nuts and, from the toe of each stocking, a new penny; we generally created such a din that our parents decided that they might as well get up. It was during such a dawn episode that Joyce ate a complete model 'Smoker's Outfit' made of chocolate and oddly enough was not sick; though Norman said she deserved to be – it was *his* 'Smoker's Outfit'!

Breakfast was always cold ham, a whole leg, covered with golden bread-crumbs, its bony end garnished with a white paper frill. Afterwards we exchanged other presents: for us, nearly always an 'Annual' of some kind and other things for which we had hopefully asked. One year my parents made a doll's house for Joyce and me from an up-ended orange box stand-ing on four legs, so that the three divisions rose one above the other and were connected by miniature staircases. Each of the three rooms so formed was carpeted with tapestry and furnished as a kitchen, living-room and bed-room; the front was left open but the whole was crowned with a gabled roof. Father usually received sweets or 'Woodbines'. He it was who on Christmas Eve would slip us a few pence to enable us to do our shopping.

After breakfast we children would be sent to church, to find, on our return, mother and father dressed and ready to go out: for Christmas Day was traditionally spent at Granny's. I always enjoyed the walk along the Iffley Road to Temple Street: there was a crispness in the air which was exciting. We passed many windows illuminated by glowing Christmas trees and coloured lights; we called 'Merry Christmas' to strangers we would have passed by during the year and we wore our new gloves and swung our new handbags with pride. We entered Granny's little terraced house to be greeted by the delicious smell of cooking bird and she had to be shown our presents and regaled with our chatter. We ate our dinner seated round her

Iffley Road, Oxford, in about 1910

oval gate-legged table covered with a cloth of pristine whiteness, against which the silver shone and the china gleamed. The meat course was followed by a pudding under which brandy had been set alight, mince pies and hot raisins soaked in brandy and ignited. After dinner came another distribution of gifts and games and competitions; if it was fine we played for a while in the garden, coming in for tea and more games until bedtime. We three children slept at Granny's, but our parents walked home in the small hours and we were returned by an aunt the following day.

Boxing Day seemed always bright and frosty, sometimes with sun, but I cannot remember rain. Our front room, littered with boxes, books and wrapping paper, was quickly tidied up by mother whilst father lit the fire. On this day relatives mostly came to our house for dinner and stayed until late evening to join in the games and partake of the food prepared by my mother: always there was a selection of blancmanges, jellies and tinned fruits, which to us were one of the treats of this festival, for they were not then in everyday supply. The table would be laid with the best white damask cloth, silver, holly-decorated paper serviettes and crackers, and the meal eaten in an atmosphere of enjoyment by the paper-hatted assembly. After dinner, mother and the lady guests coped with the mass of washing-up whilst father and the menfolk adjourned to the front room where the combined effect of food, wine, cigar smoke and a warm fire soon rendered them slumbrous so that they nodded off. I used to think this a great waste of time and often took my presents into the living-room where Norman and Joyce joined me; here we could play dice games or argue without fear of reproof.

By four o'clock mother and the others were usually 'dying for a cup of tea', but having had more than my share of nuts and sweets during the afternoon, I was not hungry and could gaze at the befrilled ice and almond-paste cake with complete indifference. But tea, a casual meal, was soon over, to be followed by games and competitions and a sing-song around the piano. My mother was adept at devising ways of presenting small gifts to our visitors, all of which meant a great deal of work beforehand but mother said it was worthwhile and, certainly, the joyful memory of Christmas has been a happy legacy to her family. All this activity subsided as the evening wore on and inevitably the table was again laid for supper of cold meat, vegetables, and the remains of puddings and mince pies. Looking back, I cannot think how I stayed the course though I must admit to having had no difficulty at the time.

Another excitement of this day after Christmas was the morning visit of the 'Mummers'. These were local men, dressed in a variety of costumes but always including Father Christmas who, in a red robe, led on a chain a man dressed as a dancing bear making playful lunges at the excited children. (This was probably a survival of the real dancing bears which toured villages and fairs in the eighteenth century.) The companions of Father Christmas rattled collecting boxes at the crowd, who gave generously in the happy spirit of the moment. I have since been told that the collection was for beer money rather than charity but, be that as it may, the show provided a memorable spectacle and a fitting conclusion to the celebration of Christmas.

# CHAPTER EIGHTEEN

# AND WE SHALL HAVE SNOW

During the months of November and December we had endured the cold promise of winter and stumbled and groped through periods of thick fog, so dense that sometimes buses were forced to stop running; or if they did manage to crawl along in bottom gear, one relied upon the conductor to call out the fare stages, and dismounted from the lighted interior into a swirling, yellow mass which rendered familiar buildings almost unrecognizable; but once Christmas was over we faced the true winter of snow and ice.

There was a great excitement about those wintry mornings, so cold that a glass of water at the bedside would be frozen solid. To wake and peer over the bedclothes with a nose already cold, at a window feather-patterned with frost, was an experience to be followed up, and at father's call upstairs: 'Hurry up! Jack Frost is about!' we lost no time in getting downstairs to the warmth of the fireside. Porridge was usually served on these mornings and this we ate under the gaslight; the curtains and window-blind still drawn as if to shield us from the cold white splendour outside. Our boots, coats, hats and gloves would be laid around the hearth to warm, for mother knew that nothing would keep us indoors on a morning like this. During hard frosts, our garden would glitter and sparkle in the cold early sunshine and the ground would be so hard that the Blakeys in the soles of our boots gave off a metallic ring as we walked; but when the snow fell, our world was transformed. Sometimes heavy snow lay in drifts up against the kitchen door so that father had to dig a way out with the coal shovel from the hearth, sprinkling this cleared path with salt or ashes from the fire. Watching this operation, I thought it a pity to spoil that beautiful white expanse which softly rounded unsightly edges and lay like a crown on the lid of the old water-butt. The black branches of the apple trees were white-trimmed as if with ermine; and when the cold wind blew, needling the face, a shower of snow eddied down on the unwary; sound was muffled, and over all hung a stillness, a sense of unreality.

Fortified by hot food and warm clothing we were out of the house at the earliest possible moment to join our friends in the street. Sometimes, if it was not a school-day, there were errands to do before play, for delivery men were reluctant to bring their horses on the slippery roads before gravelling had been done. On one occasion I saw a horse, harnessed to a cart, fall in our street, and to raise the poor animal was a very difficult matter. So we usually collected such things as bread and milk from the nearby shops and dairies. During the morning, Corporation lorries, laden with gravel, would slowly tour the streets and from the back of these, two men would shovel gravel, flinging it on to the road behind them; and although this helped, during a severe spell the centre of the roads remained covered with ruts of grey ice and frozen slush and the gutters piled with dirty snow, swept from the footpaths by householders, until the thaw. Icicles hung around blocked gutters and downstacks and along railings and from these we would select the choicest which we then sucked as a lolly.

Once the shopping was done we were free and inevitably made our way to the recreation ground. Even in winter the rec. held its attraction. Then

A late fall of snow in Howard Street in April 1908

the bare branches of the elm were etched as black filigree against the leaden sky; elderberry bush and bramble bent under the weight of snow which also covered the whole playing field like a pure white carpet. Pure, that is, until local children invaded the area: booted, gloved and woolly-hatted, with large woollen scarves crossed over the chest and tied at the back, they fell upon the snow in sheer joy. The quiet stillness of early morning was broken by their shouts and laughter, breath emerging from their mouths like so many puff-balls; and soon the white surface was pockmarked with the imprint of many small feet. Black, glossy slides appeared along the tarma-cadam path; eager hands in sodden woollen gloves collected the white mass to build a bigger and better snowman than ever before. Older boys pelted each other with snowballs from behind snow barricades and the cold and discomfort of wet hands was ignored. The frozen water of the shallow but wide ditch which separated the rec. from the allotments, crackled beneath exploratory boots, so that at the end of the day its glassy whiteness had been reduced to shattered, dirty brown fragments. By late afternoon, we were usually quite glad to get home to the warmth of a fire and the comfort of a huge pile of hot dripping toast standing in the hearth; for the snow lost its attraction as it became soiled and slushy, and clothing which had been warm and dry was now clinging uncomfortably, so that mothers found themselves with a clothes-horse draped with dripping garments which needed to be dried off before the kitchen range.

Almost without fail, every year, fields beside the river approached by Meadow Lane froze over and offered a fine opportunity for skaters. This should have been a completely free enterprise but occasionally, out-of-work men would offer to clear the snow from the expanse of ice and then charge twopence for the service.

If snow fell on a weekday, we went unwillingly to school, making the most of the journey to and fro by jumping in and out of the big drifts, so that it sometimes came over the top of our Wellington boots and we were obliged to carry always a spare pair of socks; it was a rule in school that we always changed from boots to plimsolls for indoor wear. Often when the weather was bad we took our dinner in the form of sandwiches and fruit and this we ate in the classroom. The heating in schools then was by coal fire, which almost roasted the children immediately before it, but failed to reach those sitting further back, so that lessons in the winter were most uncomfortable and concentration difficult for a small, shivering body. Sometimes we sat on our hands for warmth, or held them in our armpits, withdrawing them only when it became imperative to execute some writ-ten work, and it was with relief that we came to the end of the day and hur-ried home.

The cold weather also brought problems for householders. Water pipes froze, so that plumbers were in great demand and my father was frequently called out to restore the supply with the aid of a blowlamp, or later, with the thaw, to repair bursts. In this respect we were lucky – 'the cobbler's children were well shod'. In our house every pipe which could conceivably feel the chill wind of winter was well lagged, and the outside lavatory kept heated with paraffin lamps, the warmth and glow of which, I thought, made it quite a cosy place.

Eventually came the thaw. Soft brown slush covered streets and pavements and water gurgled fiercely along gutters and into the drains. The damp now penetrated as the cold had done and the polished red tiles of our kitchen floor were constantly awash as we tramped in and out. My mother mopped and swabbed, finally resigning herself to the mess until the weather improved. Some parts of Oxford experienced much flooding at such times, or during heavy storms, particularly in the south, but we, being on higher ground, were more fortunate, though the gardens became boggy and unworkable.

But January was also the time for parties and there was no lack of these. Norman's birthday was on 27 January, so this was made the occasion for a children's party at our house to which we each invited our friends. These were great events with sometimes as many as twenty or thirty children running all over that small house. My aunt May came down to help mother and there were jellies, blancmanges, sausage rolls, iced cakes and fruit for all. Mostly I invited girls from my class at school and in return I was invited to their houses. In addition to these private celebrations there were many children's parties organized by large business concerns. The Co-operative Wholesale Society gave huge parties often held in the town hall to which we would be taken, and from which we would be collected, by my father. For these gatherings we always wore our best party dresses and black dancing pumps, and the boys, well scrubbed and with hair slicked back with water, wore their best suits. Trestle tables covered with white paper, bon-bons, plates, mugs and party food, stretched the whole length of the main hall and back again; and the plump cherubs decorating the balcony which encircled this hall must have looked down with envy as we scrambled for places beside our friends. Bon-bons were pulled and paper hats worn, and the din subsided only temporarily during the serious business of demolishing sandwiches, jellies and high-piled plates of fruit slab cake. After tea the tables were cleared away by the stoical helpers and the games began: 'Oranges and Lemons' was entered into with great enthusiasm by a long snake of children, followed by 'Poor Mary lies a-weeping', 'I sent a letter to my love' and similar games. Then came the anticipated visit of Father Christmas and the distribution of gifts to all from the big illuminated tree which stood just below the stage, and by eight o'clock a hot, sticky and somewhat dishevelled queue of children, each clutching a bag of sweets and an orange, filed through the hall door into the foyer where parents were waiting to take them home.

In addition to the main room of the town hall there were offices and assembly rooms, all in constant use and in 1920 a revival of the Oxford Trades Exhibition was staged. Originally started in 1905, this event had lapsed during the war but local tradesmen welcomed its return and many and varied were the stalls set out to tempt customers. The main staircase leading to the hall was banked with flowers and ferns supplied and arranged

A display by Twinings at a trade fair in the Town Hall

by local florists and once inside the visitor was assailed by displays of toiletries, furniture and fashion, and invitations to sample this food or try that perfume. Our chief enjoyment was to collect literature of every commodity and free samples of products such as pencils, bookmarks and from the grocery stall individual packs of biscuits or small pots of jam. There were craftsmen displaying their skills in leather work, carpentry and building and I particularly remember a huge cake, intricately decorated with white icing as the centrepiece of a local caterer's stand. These exhibitions were well attended both by those with serious commercial intentions and those who, like ourselves, went merely for interest and fun.

Political parties also gave a treat to local children at this time. My father was a strong Conservative, but he had a friend who was an equally strong Liberal. Having no political convictions myself I was quite happy to receive invitations from both camps, which I accepted without a qualm! After tea, these parties often included a Punch and Judy show or a Magic Lantern film of the rib-tickling exploits of one, Fatty Arbuckle.

For adults there were guild socials, bring-and-buy sales, and local dramatic societies performed sketches and plays which we could attend as a family. The church and its allied organizations also provided family entertainment in the form of socials or concerts. I recall attending such a concert in the Mission Hall in Magdalen Road, being so persuaded by glowing accounts of rehearsals from a small boy named Joe, in my class at school. Joe's part, of which he was so proud, was to pop up from a box at a given signal, with the words: 'I'm Jack-in-the-box'. But Joe was too eager, too impatient, and popped up three times before he should, completely ruining the intended surprise of his appearance!

The jollity promised by all this activity was not allowed, in the minds of women, to detract from the appeal of the January sales. In the opening days of the month, long queues formed in early morning at the entrances to haberdashery shops which, when their doors opened, were besieged by jostling customers anxious to find cheap articles with which to replenish their linen cupboards. An advertisement of 1926 reads:

| | |
|---|---|
| Cotton sheets (double) | 10/11d –25/6d per pair. |
| Pure linen sheets (double) | 45/11d reduced to 29/11d in sale. |
| Witney blankets (double) | 1 pair 27/11d sale offer. |
| Linen pillow cases | 2/6½d each, in sale. |
| Large white bath towels | 3/6d each. |

For the menfolk there were slashing reductions in the furniture, hardware and gardening stores and the glowing offers made in newspapers by mail order firms kept up the pressure.

To the shopkeepers the sales provided an opportunity to clear their shelves of old stock and replace with new and for the customer there was the thrill, however deluded, of a bargain, of some new possession, for it was generally agreed that 'a change is as good as a rest'.

CHAPTER NINETEEN

# THE STREET STILL
# LIVES

The restless spirit of change was in the air during the year 1926. There was much talk about the regrouping of Oxford schools, the possible outcome of which was summarized by the vicar of SS Mary and John as follows:

> As far as the East Oxford Church schools are concerned this would mean that our Boys' and Girls' schools would be grouped with the Cowley Fathers' Boys' and Girls' schools. Children up to eleven would all come to SS. Mary and John schools after leaving the Infants' and from eleven to fourteen they would go to the Cowley Fathers' schools, unless they went to a Central School.

However, before this reorganization could be effected, in the early months of 1927, I sat my scholarship examinations. These were held in various schools throughout the county but I took mine in South Oxford school situated in St Aldate's. There were two examinations, followed by an interview, of which I remember only one question:

'And what is your father's occupation?'

'He is a plumber.'

'And what does that involve?'

'He mends taps.'

Exactly what effect this exchange had on my assessment I shall never know, but I was accepted and allocated to the Oxford Central Girls' School in New Inn Hall Street, which pleased my family very much. My brother had, a few years previously, obtained a place at the Oxford Wesleyan Higher Grade School for boys, in the same street and mother thought that we would now be able to travel to school together on the bus so that my brother could keep an eye on my safety. Needless to say, this idea soon fell apart, Norman naturally preferring the company of his friends, but as my best friend was also to start at my school we travelled together and no difficulty arose. Often we walked to and fro, thus saving our bus fares; some weeks I managed to save 1s. 3d. by this method.

From the outset it was instilled in me that to be a 'Central' girl brought with it a certain prestige and behaviour responsibilities. It was impressed upon all pupils that both in and out of the classroom, in and out of uniform, the good name of the school was to be our first thought. Pushing in queues, showing-off in shops or buses, loud conversation or walking more than two abreast in the streets was forbidden and offenders reported by local shopkeepers or vigilant prefects were given a severe reprimand by the

Silver Jubilee party in Catherine Street in 1935. Many of these children would have been known by the author

headmistress in a manner not quickly forgotten. Often we chafed against what we regarded as a tyrannical ruling, but we nevertheless took heed and in later, wiser years, appreciated its purpose.

Attendance at this school represented a big step in my life away from the familiar confines of our street; I made new friends and found new experiences in a wider horizon, but this is all part of a natural growing-up process and not to be regretted. Eventually my parents moved away from the area and for many years our lives were concerned with pastures new.

Yet nostalgia affects us all from time to time and I am no exception. I have recently been back to my old haunts to find many changes, some for better, some for worse.

The Withy brook no longer sparkles and ripples over stepping stone and pebble, but flows dully and uninterestingly through culvert and channel, and the allotments are fast disappearing beneath brick and concrete. The lane to the ferry is completely overgrown and lost to this generation, though it would serve no purpose, for the ferry-boat has been replaced by the Donnington Bridge over which children, on foot or cycle, make their way to Long Bridges. The bathing-place has been opened up; the corrugated iron barrier separating boys and girls has been removed and the area pleasantly landscaped for all to share.

The towpath, now neatly edged in concrete, follows a river mostly frequented by steamers and motor-launches; the humble punt appears to have been relegated to the safer and quieter waters of the Cherwell.

The lock has lost some of its appeal, for it is now mechanically controlled, but the sight of so many boats gathered to pass through it does still attract and interest people of all ages.

Progress has also left its mark on those much-loved fields which lie beyond the lock, but my eyes, pricked by hot tears, did not see the by-pass which now scars the skyline, nor my ears register the whine of traffic which hurtles along its length. I saw only a wilted bunch of buttercups and clover, and I heard only the echo of a child's laughter. For me at least, there are still snakesheads and yellow iris to be found on the far side of those fields where the land lies marshy; gnats still dance above the cowpats, and the season is always summer.

I retain, too, my respect for the rushing waters of the weir, pausing to study its turbulence from the safety of the little bridge which spans it and at the end of which stands the toll-house now padlocked, neglected and undemanding.

I am reassured by the light and shade cast by the sun on the grey stone charm of Iffley. Bees busy themselves about the clumps of purple aubretia clinging to its garden walls and, come September, the big chestnut tree by the churchyard wall will again spill its brown, shiny fruit into the roadway;

but the village has grown and many of the beautiful trees at the Turn have been felled to make way for house building.

The grassy bank verges of the main Cowley Road have given way to tarmacadam path and kerbing, and the wild hedgerows which once lined its route have been replaced by the neatly trimmed privet and flower borders of modern homes.

There have been changes, too, in our street. I have sauntered along those well-trodden footpaths meeting not a soul I knew, seeing not a face I recognized. Strange curtains hang in once familiar windows; and front railings, removed by government order to aid our efforts in the Second World War have been replaced by a variety of fences and walls. No children play in the roadway, for it is a busy thoroughfare, and the gutters where our marbles once rolled are scored with continuous yellow lines, but, at the time of my visit, on our front gate step sat a little boy, bright of eye and dark of skin.

The old church of St Alban with its hideous corrugated-iron extensions was demolished in 1932 and the much-admired figure of its patron saint is now housed in a pleasant modern building, light, airy and beautifully maintained.

Most of the little corner shops have disappeared, crushed by supermarket and chain-store, and the bakery has exchanged its warm comforting smell for the stink of petrol with cars housed in the space once occupied by crusty loaves.

The Green is hidden beneath a squat building bearing a sign 'Slipper Baths', stifling with its very foundations those years of squabble and laughter; and the rec., the space that was ours, had become a vast housing estate even before we left.

But the people I did see, many of varied origins, appeared happy and certainly more prosperous than in my day. They are reconstructing and renovating the old houses with worthy diligence; for the street is now their world, the scene of their daily toil and preoccupation in which I play no part.

Any comparison I may make, any regret I may have, is coloured by memories of a happy childhood. Whether my parents, who had to cope with the difficulties of those times, would so cherish the old days is another matter.

So, of what use is nostalgia? The street still lives and I must be content.

# BIBLIOGRAPHY

Alexander, Sally, *St. Giles Fair 1830–1914,* Oxford, Ruskin College, 1970.

Bickerton, Fred, *Fred of Oxford,* London, Evans, 1953.

Blair, *Oxford Ways,*Oxford, Blackwell, 1925.

Burgon, The Very Revd J.W., *May Morning on Magdalen Tower,* Oxford, Alden, *c.* 1883.

Butler, C.V., *Social Conditions in Oxford,* London, Sidgwick & Jackson, 1912.

Cordrey, Edward, *Bygone Days at Iffley,* Oxford, 1956.

Cowley St John parish magazines, 1920–6.

Graham, Malcolm, *Henry Taunt of Oxford,* Oxford, Oxford Illustrated Press, 1973.

Graham, Malcolm, *On Foot in Oxford, No. 2: Cowley,* Oxford, Oxford City Libraries, 1973.

Graham, Malcolm, *On Foot in Oxford, No. 3: St Clements & East Oxford,* Oxford, Oxfordshire County Libraries, 1974.

Huggett, F.E., *A Day in the Life of a Victorian Farmworker,* London, Allen & Unwin, 1972.

Judge, C.W., *Oxford Past and Present,* Oxford, Oxford Illustrated Press, 1970.

Mallinson, The Revd Arnold, *Quinquagesimo Anno,* Oxford, Dugdale, 1974.

Muncey, R.W., *Old English Fairs,* London, Sheldon Press, 1935.

*Oxford Diocesan Year Book,* 1975.

Paintin, Harry, *Magdalen Tower and May Morning,* Oxford, Oliver, 1914.

Parkes, G.D., & Mary, *May Day at Iffley,* Oxford, OUP, 1934.

Robb-Smith, Dr A.H.T., *A Short History of Radcliffe Infirmary,* Oxford, United Oxford Hospitals, 1970.

Samuel, R. (ed.), *Village Life and Labour,* London, Routledge, 1975.

The *Silver Jubilee Book,* London, Odhams Press, 1935.

Taunt, H.W., *Iffley Manor, Church and Village,* Oxford, Taunt, 1909.

Taunt, H.W., 'May Day Ceremonies', *The Sphere,* 2 May 1908.

Taunt, H.W., *St. Giles Fair, the popular Oxford carnival, and its story,* Oxford, Taunt, 1906.

*Victoria History of the County of Oxford,* Vol. 2, (ed.) William Page, London, Constable, 1907.

*Victoria History of the County of Oxford,* Vol. 5, (ed.) M.D. Lobel, London, OUP, 1959.